For Christopher McCoy
gypsy moth, missionary, ardent lover of maps, geography,
Peru and all strange lands, Early Fathers of the Church,
and the poor, especially of Villa Salvador, Lima.
Dedicated passionately to the Mystery,
the Kingdom's enduring justice, peace and truth.
My home in Liverpool, web connection to Wales
and England and anywhere else we can go,
who feeds me images, books and unfinished stories,
gleefully corrects my English and translates for me.
Best at laughing as he disappears right before my eyes!
Mil gracias, mi amigo, de mi corazón.

"Growth does not come from putting on any spiritual clothing. Growth comes from removing and removing, ceasing, undoing, and letting ourselves drop down or even fall into the core of our living being."

—Linda Hogan
Chickasaw poet
quoted in *Listening to the Land*

LENT:
THE SUNDAY READINGS

LENT:
THE SUNDAY READINGS

Reflections and Stories

Megan McKenna

ORBIS BOOKS

Maryknoll, New York 10545

The Catholic Foreign Mission Society of America (Maryknoll) recruits and trains people for overseas missionary service. Through Orbis Books, Maryknoll aims to foster the international dialogue that is essential to mission. The books published, however, reflect the opinions of their authors and are not meant to represent the official position of the society.

Published by Orbis Books, Maryknoll, NY 10545-0308
Manufactured in the United States of America
Manuscript editing and typesetting by Joan Marie Laflamme

ORBIS/ISBN 1-57075-102-1

Contents

THE TRIDUUM

CYCLE A

Nuestro Salvador de las Sandias

Introduction

The first cycle of readings is the primary set of scripture passages for Lent. These readings are used whenever the community initiates new members at the Easter Vigil and celebrates the sacraments of baptism, confirmation, and eucharist. These readings are catecumenate lessons, gleaned from the early church's experience of how to "make" new Christians. Their overall theme is one that all Christians need to be reminded of yearly: We live now no longer for ourselves alone, but we live now hidden with Christ in God. We have died with Christ; we have been buried with Christ; and we live in resurrection glory with Christ. All of us who have been baptized into Christ now live by the power of the Holy Spirit with Jesus to the glory of God the Father. The season of Lent renews the whole church, calling it to a more fervent devotion, a holy resistance to evil, a more single-hearted lifestyle, purer worship, a more encompassing sacrifice, and deeper communion among the members of the body of Christ.

The readings of the first two Sundays find us with Jesus in the desert, driven there by the power of the Spirit to be tempted and tested by Satan. This is a time to be seen and known for who we are and what we claim to be—the sons and daughters of God. It is a public call to witness to our faithfulness individually as a community of believers. It signals the need for alertness, true worship, and wholehearted trust in God that must characterize the weeks of Lent.

In these days we face down evil nonviolently and learn once again how to live with holy resistance to sin; we cling to the presence of God in the person of Jesus the Christ. The battle lines are drawn. The readings draw the parameters of where and how we will stand together with Jesus against Satan, the Hinderer, and all that keeps us from living in the freedom of the children of God that we pledged in our baptisms.

The second Sunday lifts our spirits and heartens our bodies and souls. We journey up the mountain of the transfiguration with Jesus, Peter, James, and John, our companions in prayer. It is a moment of vision and insight and glory. It is a time to ponder and reflect on who Jesus is for us, for our community of believers, and for the universal church.

We are privileged to see in Jesus the Messiah, the light of the world, the Son of Man, the Savior, the beloved Son of God. We are commanded by God the Father to attend to the Word of God made flesh in the person of Jesus, for that is an absolute necessity if we are to come through the trials of Lent to the fullness of Easter's glory, if we are to die to ourselves so as to live in the redeeming presence of the risen Lord.

It is a time to gather to discuss our insights and belief, to talk among ourselves about the mystery of resurrection for Jesus and in our own lives. We are exhorted to follow Jesus as he calls us to go with him on his way to Jerusalem.

The final three readings from John's gospel form the core of the cycle A readings. They are primary catechetical texts that take the baptismal candidates and the community of believers through the process of faith. The story of the woman at the well details what it means to believe in Jesus and to witness to others confessing both our sin and our faith, sharing that experience with others as good news. The story of the man born blind extends this process to one who is called not just to believe in Jesus but to become a disciple and to experience persecution for being associated with Jesus, the Truth incarnate.

Finally, there is the story of the raising of Lazarus from the dead by the power of the Word of the Lord, who calls him forth from the tomb and commands the community to unbind him and set him free to live the life of resurrection. Lazarus and all of us who have been baptized are dangerous to the world because others will come to belief because of what God has done for us in Jesus.

This three-week primer on growth in belief brings us to Holy Week, where we are invited to take the way of the cross with Jesus, obedient and trusting in God the Father. We are to call down forgiveness even on those who stand against us and revile us because we stand with Jesus, who is the Way, the Truth, and the Life. In the end, Passion Week gathers our lives together and hands them over as thanksgiving, as sacrifice made holy with Jesus, and we are taken and held with care in the heart of God the Father. These readings express the heart of what it means to be in the company of Jesus, to live more truly in the freedom of the children of God.

Sunday of the First Week of Lent

Genesis 2:7-9, 3:1-7
Romans 5:12-19
Matthew 4:1-11

For this first Sunday of Lent we go back to our beginnings, our roots in a garden, and we are exhorted to remember who we are, where we came from, how it was originally meant to be, and how we changed the story. The story begins with God forming the first human being, Adam, out of the ground itself and bending to breathe into Adam the life of God. And Adam became alive, with breath! Life is shared, passed on. We are born with the exhalation and inspiration of God close to us. Home is a garden full of plants and trees, two especially that are gifts of presence, pleasing to the eye like the others, but not necessarily good to eat. These are the tree of life and the tree of the knowledge of good and evil. It is a good beginning.

But the story moves off to a serpent, not God, but still created by God. This one approaches the woman and insinuates, questions her: "Did God really say you must not eat from any tree in the garden?" The question posits a Creator who baits those with whom Divine life was shared. It insults God. The woman answers, logically and truthfully, that it's only of the tree in the middle of the garden that they are not supposed to eat, because if they do they will die.

The serpent is cunning. He begins by separating the two, questioning only one, so that they cannot rely on one another. Then he lies, twisting the words so that they sound reasonable and are partially correct—disfiguring and maiming the very words of God. Now the serpent contradicts God, adding to the insult, insinuating that God is a liar. "You won't die. God knows that the day you eat it, you'll both be like gods yourself." Humanity will know good and evil both; know how to be human, made in the image of God, and how to be inhuman, marring and scarring that image beyond recognition.

She looks, sees, eats, and then shares the fruit of the tree with her husband, who now joins her in the endeavor. Their eyes are opened, and they do see. The first thing they see is that they are naked—self-conscious, aware of separation, difference, distance. They have listened to words not of God and acted on them—and the story goes off kilter, careening out of control. From here on the Creator will have to be more and more imaginative and inventive in order to keep the story full of life, for now death has taken root in the story.

What's done is done. The consequences will seep through the history of the garden, exile, and all the earth. The trees are still there—the tree of life and the tree of the knowledge of good and evil. Our heritage is both good and evil, and we are passionately exhorted that no matter how much we now know of evil, we must choose good. It is imperative for humanity that we choose the good.

The segment of Paul's letter to the Romans couches this primeval story in legalistic terms of sin, death, law, disobedience, fault and compensation for sin, condemnation of the sinners, transgression, and the sentence of death. It's rather depressing. But the language is alternated with the theology of grace and gift, which is pardon that ever more abounds in the face of sin.

The comparison is between the first human being, Adam the transgressor, and Jesus Christ, who is righteous and holy and just before God and who makes us friends of God once again. But, basically, it reminds us that grace is stronger than death, that God is more gracious than anything we could hope for, and that God is generous in gifting us with the presence of Jesus Christ, who brings forgiveness for sin into the story and so makes possible another ending besides condemnation and death for all sinners, for all human beings. In Jesus, and the reign of God that comes with his presence in the world, comes life. The reign of death is broken. Now what does the story say? What marvelous possibilities and choices lie ahead for those who grasp hold of their freedom as the sons and daughters of God?

Traditionally the readings for the first Sunday of Lent are accounts of Jesus in the desert struggling with Satan. After the struggle he sets his face toward Jerusalem and chooses the way that will lead invariably to the cross and resurrection. We are to listen to Jesus with ears open to the truth—as opposed to listening to the serpent, Satan. We are told again to choose, but now we have a story to hear and attend to: the story of the One who chooses rightly, freely, gracefully, and so redeems the tale.

This story of Jesus being tested in the desert is a model for all Christians who will more consciously deal with temptations, sin, and evil—and choices in regard to these issues—in the next six weeks. It is an example of behavior that shows us how to resist, how to chose rightly, how to become again the children of God.

Sin is the temptation not to act as sons and daughters of God, the temptation not to obey the Word and not to respond to the commands of God. Jesus is seen in the desert, alone with Satan, and Satan is trying to find out who Jesus is—is he the Son of God? The answer is revealed not just in words but in Jesus' obedience to the word of the Lord in the scriptures.

Jesus and Satan interpret scripture in vastly different ways. Satan—the word means "the hinderer"—is anyone, anything, any interpretation of reality, or religion, any relationship or situation or philosophy that hinders us from being the children of God, from sharing in the breath of God, life itself, or hinders others from recognizing that life within us.

Satan interprets scripture in bits and pieces, out of context, trying to use the word for his own benefit or knowledge. Jesus, on the other hand, sees all of scripture as one piece, a holistic call to integrity that defends the honor of God and situates all choices in a balanced framework that calls us to obedience and humility.

In Matthew's account the first temptation is to make bread from stones. The second is to jump from the top of the Temple, thus baiting God to prove the Divine love by saving us from being human, from suffering and death. The last temptation is to use the ways of the world, where power and authority belong to Satan and those with whom he chooses to share his kingdoms, as the way to bring the kingdom of God on earth.

The passage is layered with meaning and includes basic reminders of how to deal with life's temptations and inclinations toward evil. The scriptures tell us how to live if they are interpreted correctly, meaning if they are used to inspire us to respond as Jesus did. First, we live as Christians, on every word that comes forth from the mouth of God. Second, we do not put the Lord our God to the test. Rather, it is God who tests our faithfulness, our righteousness in the daily situations of life, history, society, family, and church.

There is suffering, pain, and death to contend with. Our relationship with God as our Father, Jesus as our Brother, and the Spirit as our strength and guide protects us, but it does not save us from pain. It does, however, reveal God's will in every situation, especially in pain, injustice, suffering, and death. God does take care of us in hard times, during persecution and the ordinary course of human life and death, but not in superhuman ways; rather, God cares for us by companionship, hope, faith, and sustaining grace. Our religion teaches us to obey God and bend before God alone, to live humanly in the face of consequences that reek of death and despair. Jesus obeyed even in the face of rejection, the cross, and death.

The third temptation is about worship, where we surrender to and submit to power. There is only One to surrender to if you are a child of God. Homage is for God alone and not to the world's ways of money, power, prestige, security, fortune, fame, authority, a place in society at the cost of others, selfishness, or violence.

The three encounters between Satan and Jesus are a three-pronged attack on evil as it creeps into our lives. They reveal the three things most helpful in repelling evil: the study and practice of the scriptures; faithfulness in the midst of suffering and death (including penance and fasting and almsgiving); and the true worship of God that is integral to government, family, church, society, and personal lives. God must be served in every area of life—that is the kingdom of God and how it comes.

Lent is a time to take back the pieces of our lives that have been given over to authorities other than God. It is a time to do homage to God alone, and it is a time, too, when angels will come and wait on us, a time of challenge, choices, failures, promises, change, small victories, and a deepened awareness of how much we must grow still in the Christian life. It is a time of trust, with the season of the cross shadowing us.

The cross is the symbol of salvation, of the gifts of mercy and justice, of the truth of how much we are loved and trusted by God. It is in these days that we turn toward the cross in hope and begin to obey Jesus' call to discipleship more intently and wholeheartedly. Our cross is our share in both the practice of injustice and evil of the world and our share in the sufferings of Christ to restore the world and weave all of creation back into an integral body that worships God and lives in thanksgiving. Lent is for putting the world back together again; we are joined with Jesus as he pulls the world back into relationship with God in his own flesh and blood and bone and we share in that work in our bodies too.

These stories of Genesis and the beginning of Matthew's gospel tell the truth of why the world is the way it is, why evil is among us and laced seemingly in the very bones and patterns of our mind, why disobedience seems stronger than goodness, why we do evil, why we affect one another so strongly, why we sense this terrible separation from God and one another, why the world seems to be falling apart, and, lastly, why God created us. They obviously cover a lot.

Sometimes Genesis and other fragments of the gospel are called myth. Theologians and storytellers say that a myth never happened because it is still in process. It is not finished; it is still happening now. So, these stories are not just about beginnings but about the present, now, in our lives and inconsistencies and disobediences, our broken relationships and separations, our searches for wisdom, eternal life, and a relationship with God and one another that is whole and life sustaining. We have all sinned, and we all do sin and encourage others to sin—all in varying degrees. We are human and responsible for the earth and one another. The stories are not just about individuals: Adam and Eve or Jesus. They are stories about all human beings and the roots that we share in common.

We have all shared in the sting of the serpent. In ancient and medieval times this sting of sin, lies, and death was symbolized by a scorpion. In 1 Corinthians 15:54-55 we read: "Death is swallowed up in victory, Where, O death, is your victory? Where, O death, is your sting?" In many Spanish countries and neighborhoods there is the custom of making a large papier-mâché scorpion (with six legs and a stinger) to signify the sting of death. Each week, one leg is hacked off. The stinger is cut off in Holy Week. On Easter Eve, fire from the Easter fire is brought home and the scorpion is set on fire and destroyed, as in the life, death, and resurrection of Jesus. Lent is about stopping the sting, about destroying death, and about uncrucifying the world.

The telling of the desert temptations is a good place to begin our testing, to see where we are weak, or need help or strengthening. This examination of conscience can be used in conjunction with the three temptations and with the readings that follow in this first week of Lent.

- What feeds me (that is not the Word of God)?
- What do I use to avoid conflict?
- How do I avoid being vulnerable (hungry) in my life?
- Do I take care of my needs and feelings first?
- In times of hardship or depression do I remember to look to scripture for help, comfort, directions, remedies?
- Do I use the things of the earth wisely, for what they were created, or do I use them for what I want?
- Do I violently try to change others or situations for my immediate needs?
- Do I try to prove to others who I am by what I do in public?
- Do I worship the ways of the world instead of God, or besides God?

- Do I use money, reputation, or power to change things instead of changing myself?
- Do I look for answers to my life in society's values and morals rather than trying to live up to the demands of the gospel?
- Do I "sell my soul" to get what I want?
- Do I rely on my privileged relationship with God (as son or daughter) to protect me from harm, from being human, from suffering and dying?
- Do I use God to reassure myself that I'm okay?
- Do I act like I'm a god with others?
- Do I obey God's commands, remembering that I am human and need to learn discipline and practice if I am to be a follower?
- Am I always trying to get ahead and move up in society?
- Do I trust God to take care of me and my family and so spend time working for the kingdom and taking care of the people who are poor and less fortunate than I?

Lent is a time to look at our weaknesses and failures and work on changing so that we can help others. It is a time of mutual encouragement and strengthening. This exercise of freedom, of making choices, is a gift of God. We can bring hope to the story, to others' stories, and to the story of the universe too. The following story—sometimes called "Is the King Ready Yet?"—may help us to go through this week with courage, daring to take risks for the truth and life.

✢ Once upon a time there was a king, a good and just man, who struggled to bring peace to his land. One day as he stood listening to a master preaching he resolved to leave his kingdom behind him and become the master's follower. Soon after, he presented himself before the master and asked to become his disciple. The master looked hard at him and finally spoke, "You were once a king. It is not going to be easy for you to become a disciple, a servant of all." The king stood silent.

   The master looked at him again and spoke again, "However, I will take you on a probationary basis. I will assign tasks to you, and when I think you are ready I will make you a disciple. Are you willing to obey me and learn how to be a disciple by unlearning how to be a king?" The king heartily agreed, for this was to be his life from now on.

With that, the king was welcomed into the group. Immediately, the master assigned him to the most lowly, humiliating task of collecting the garbage and slop pails three times a day.

The king, now a follower, joined the daily round of work and prayer, study and lessons, discipline and assigned tasks. He did his onerous job faithfully, without complaining. And as the days passed many of the other disciples began to be bothered by the daily ritual of seeing this man, once their king, now reduced to such work. Finally a group of them approached the master on his behalf. "Master," they asked, "isn't the king ready yet? After all, he has been obedient and never once complained about his role."

The master simply responded, "No, he's not ready yet."

But they pleaded his case and finally the master said that he would send his number one disciple to test him and see if he was ready truly to enter into discipleship. The disciple was summoned and commanded to test the king.

Obediently the disciple set off to look for the former king. He found him walking across the marble floors of the main hall, carefully carrying his slop pails. The disciple waited for him to come closer. When the two men stood facing one another, the disciple shoved the king hard, causing him to drop the pails and spill the slops all over the clean and waxed floor. There was a long silence, and then the king looked hard at the man, his face red and the veins pulsing in his neck. He barely withheld the fury inside as he spoke: "You are lucky that I am no longer a king or else I would have had you severely punished. But I am not, so you can get away with this." With that, he went about the task of cleaning up the mess and then went back to cleaning the hall.

The disciple returned to the master and reported what had happened. The master turned to the others and said: "See, I told you he wasn't ready."

Weeks and months went by, and the other disciples watched the king day after day clean up the slops and garbage and empty the chamber pots, and they respected him for his faithfulness. After all, they had only been poor and their lot had been bettered by joining the master, but he had been king and had sunk so low.

Finally, they again approached the master—the group interceding on the king's behalf having grown much larger. They pointed out to the master that he *must* be ready now. The master looked calmly at them and said— "He isn't ready yet." They pleaded to have the disciple test him again. And so a second time the disciple went to the main hall and waited for the king.

They met in the same place as before and eyed one another.

The disciple moved quickly and once again shoved the king, causing him to drop the buckets again. This time the king looked at him, the anger burning in his eyes, but he held his tongue—though his feelings showed in the tenseness of his face and body. The disciple reported back to the master, and the master turned to the others saying, "See, I told you he wasn't ready yet."

Months passed and the other disciples grew to know and admire the king and to become friends with him. He was courteous, reflective, honest, and patient. He never spoke of his humiliating tasks or the treatment he had received at the hands of the head disciple or the fact that the master seemed to ignore him completely. Many new recruits had come to the group and had been welcomed without any stipulations. No one was asked to dump the slop pots or take the king's job.

Again, the group approached the master. This time they didn't ask. They were adamant: "Send the disciple and test him. We know he's ready." So once again the disciple went to the hall and waited for the king to come with his daily burden. They stood face to face again, and the disciple shoved him, hard, and the pots went flying off, spilling all over the floor. There was silence and the king looked mildly at the disciple and said and did nothing. Then the disciple shoved him again, almost causing him to lose his balance. And this time the king smiled and bowed respectfully to the disciple.

The disciple returned and reported it to the master. The master looked at the other disciples and said, "Now he's ready." They rejoiced.

But then the master turned and looked hard at his head disciple and spoke. "Go," he said, "and return to the hall. Find the man who once was king and tell him to come to me. You take over his job, for now you are on probation and he is now the head disciple!" Stunned, the long-time disciple moved to obey, his heart and mind in a turmoil about the turn of events.

The story is one of testing and discipleship, of learning to follow and to obey, and especially of discerning who and what we are, in all circumstances. The time is Lent. It is time to find out: Are we ready yet? Are we disciples of the Master who has gone before us into the desert, into life, death, and resurrection?

Sunday of the Second Week of Lent

Genesis 12:1-4
2 Timothy 1:8-10
Matthew 17:1-9

"Abraham was seventy-five years old when he left Haran." This seems like an add-on, a detail tagged onto the promise of the covenant that sets in motion the driving force of God's history in the world. But it is crucial. This reading notes Abraham's obedience to the command to "go forth from his own house," the house of his ancestors and his past, and it records his birth into another reality. His name changes from

Abram to Abraham. His future will be built on words and dreams, the vision of humanity redeemed and once again living together with God, as it was meant in the beginning.

Abram begins to live at seventy-five. Everything up to this time was preparation. I used to take heart from the life of St. Teresa of Avila, telling myself not to worry because nothing of real significance happened in Teresa's spiritual life apparently until after she was fifty years old. Now Abram's life and the life of a people in faith begins at seventy-five. Obviously, time with Yahweh is a different thing altogether than just consecutive years or an accumulation of experiences. Something else is seeded in history, and faith draws it forth on its own schedule. There is always something else going on beside, in, through, over, and under historical time. There is another perspective to life for one who believes in the words of God.

These words are the future of the human race, of the meaning between God and Abram—and so between all those who come after, who stake their lives on something as intangible as a covenant, a promise for their children and their children's children, willing themselves to be bound to a future of hope. These people become a blessing for all the peoples of the earth, people who live in community, with shared possibilities and pasts held in common. It seems, as with Abraham at seventy-five, that it is never too late to begin something earth-shattering and momentous with this God of ours!

The word *blessing* is repeated, as though it is a mantra, a word fraught with power in itself. It is something that God speaks, both sets in motion and accomplishes. It is also a reality already in existence that seems to have a life of its own. It is what God does and what we become and what all others on earth will recognize and take heart from, finding in this new creation humanity's redemption and the grasping of once-lost possibilities. We will be the blessing. We are re-created by the word of God. We become the blessing of God, a sigh that drifts over the world and seeps into all things and time. Eventually it will take us all home.

This Sunday, the Sunday of Transfiguration, is a day of blessing, hope, and promises made and remembered and perceived now in a person who is the blessing of God on the human race: Jesus, beloved of God. On the second Sunday of Lent we are blessed with an experience of God's continuing meaning of blessing. As Daniel Berrigan says: "Religious experience is at its root an experience of an unconditional and unrestrained being in love." The covenant says that God is unrestrainedly and unconditionally in love with us, and all of time is for us to learn its patterns in our flesh and blood so the world can breathe easier and live in hope.

Lent is for learning that we are one in Christ, that our communities are blessings for others when we believe and obey like Abram, no matter what age we begin.

Counterpoint to age and the past is Paul's letter to young Timothy and its exhortation to the future and all it holds for us. "Bear your share of the hardship which the gospel entails." This is our response, like Abram's obedience to the command to leave behind his former life, and it is based on a promise of God. Timothy and all of us are reminded that we are called to a "holy life" according to God's own design—the grace of God held out to us in Christ Jesus. This is the heart of today's readings and the meaning, the depth charge, of the story of the transfiguration: in the appearance of Christ Jesus, our Savior, not just on the mount where they go to pray together, but in history, God has robbed death of its power and has brought life and immortality.

All the words of God are about life, not bound only by time and history but by love revealed in everlasting life for all. The gospel is the covenant in flesh and blood, the person and abiding power of Jesus, who shatters history with his appearance. We live now in the shadow of Jesus, in the same Spirit that gave life to creation and reanimates all life with outrageous hope. We are saved by hope, by joyfully bearing our share of the hardships that this gospel entails. The word *bear* is core to the meaning of what Timothy and all of us as disciples are being told to grasp hold of. A woman bears a child, bringing it forth in hard labor, carrying it to its fullness and readiness to emerge into history. That bearing stops time momentarily. All that is possible is to bear the pain in hopes of a child's cry bursting forth with the pushing forth of life into history, from one world to another.

The gospel entails hardship, hard work, labor that will end in glory, in birthing a new life, a new world of hope. The message of this Sunday of Lent is not easy, but it has all the wild possibilities of Abram being told he and Sarai will have children out of time and of Jesus being raised from the dead, shattering the pattern of birth, life and death forever. Thomas Traherne, in *Centuries of Meditations*, puts it poetically, teasing out the endless possibilities we are to bear in mind as we go through time, especially these forty days:

> The cross is the abyss of wonders,
> the center of desires, the school of virtues,
> the house of wisdom, the throne of love.
> the theatre of joys and the place of sorrows;
> It is the root of happiness, and the gate of
>   heaven.

When dealing with God we must remember that we never get just what we are expecting, we always get more than we bargained for. Although God lives in "no time," we join the presence of God in time through our share in the life of Christ Jesus, given to us in baptism. Our hardships are not vague but usually very specific: obeying the laws of the church consistently; defending all life, not just the life of chosen ones that are deemed deserving; instilling Christian values into our communities and children and practicing them ourselves in the face of contradictory values of American society; supporting the church; critiquing society; defending belief; being faithful; facing suffering and hardships with trust in God and without bitterness and blame; reconciling and forgiving and clinging to forgiveness as God's gracious presence; being truthful and without rancor when the church and members of the church fail personally and collectively; and often doing penance that atones for our own and others' lack of obedience to the gospel and to the needs of those clamoring to us in history as believers in Jesus' good news to the poor.

Jesus, in the gospel, is intent on sharing this time. this experience of God, with his friends. It is a traditional account of glory and resurrection, out of time, prior to the experience of the cross. It is the story of the saved, the redeemed, inserted as hope into the season of Lent, the season of springing forth into newness of life, into the saving grace of believers' time. It is a reminder of hardship and the reality of death that is laced through the reality of resurrection. We are saved. The resurrection is a reality in our lives now, because the cross and resurrection and continual life of Jesus are with us still. It is a bolstering of spirits for the next five weeks. It is a scene of glory, awe, and reverence, a glimpse of who Jesus really is, human and obeying God, preaching the gospel, caring for the poor, bringing others back from the dead, unraveling history's hold, even if he is hidden from view for now. Our lives—our efforts and repentance and emptying out of our old life—are hidden from view as well.

God reveals Jesus in this account witnessed by Peter, James, and John, his disciples and friends. It encourages them and gives them heart. It is given to us, his disciples and friends, as well. Jesus announces to his disciples the reality of what time and history will do to him and all of us— seek to destroy us—yet God the Father will raise the Son of Man from the dead and will repay each according to his or her deeds. The Son of Man will come in glory in the kingdom of God. This is a promise.

Jesus is seen in this glory, as radiant as light, as the sun of justice, along with Moses and Elijah. These men have transcended history as hope for their people: liberator of slaves, giver of the law, prophet, words of God in the mouth of human beings. Both have deaths that seemingly defy time. No one knows when Moses died or where he was buried. God and the angels buried him, and the grave is kept secret. Elijah disappeared in a fiery chariot, borne to heaven. He is to reappear when the world is ready for the Messiah to fill time and history so completely that all the earth will know that justice and peace dwells with a people and that God visits the people once again. All history comes together in this one person, Jesus.

Peter wants to stay in this moment and place and not face the promise of the cross and suffering and death. He does not really believe in the future. He wants to stay in the present. He wants to build booths, create monuments. He is already figuring out how to use this, keep this, as we often do with experiences of God, rather than let it escort him into the future transformed. But the voice that spoke at Jesus' baptism interrupts Peter, and us, trying to get us back on track—the track of hope and promise, the track of obedience and worship. "This is my beloved son on whom my favor rests. Listen to him."

It's that simple: Listen to him and no one else in history. The disciples fall forward on their faces, flat on the ground, overcome with fear and awe, out of time, in the presence of the Holy. Then Jesus comes forward again into their lives and ordinary time and lays a hand on them saying: "Get up, do not be afraid." These few words are the essence of resurrection life: Arise and live without fear of death, the end of time, hate, injustice, suffering. We have been given the life of the Son of Man to sustain us in this history that serves God's time and promises.

When they look up again, they see only Jesus. That's the core, the heart of all history and of all life, only Jesus and what he brings into this world. On the way down the mountain Jesus commands them, in the same vein as Abram was commanded to leave his past behind, "Do not tell anyone of the vision until the Son of Man rises from the dead," that is, until the seemingly impossible becomes reality.

This account is an intimation of Easter five weeks from now. We are weak-hearted and basically timid and fearful folk and oftentimes, even by the second week of Lent, we're ready to give up. This Sunday is for courage, blessing, encouragement, and a moment of prayer, an experience of the glory of the Lord, of revelation for all us faint-hearted folk. It is for us when we act like Peter, wanting it easy, wanting to stay with glory, wanting to stay with our limited and oftentimes off-base assumptions about what is going on. It is a time for God to interrupt and once again tell us: "This is my beloved on whom my favor rests—the favor of grace, spirit, justice, care for the poor, obedience. *Listen* to him and not to anyone else."

We are called to redirect attention to Jesus, the central point of everything—the Law; the prophets; Old Testament hopes, covenants, stories, and history. All is pinned on him, his life and his response to God. His life and death and resurrection are the result of his trust and belief in God and his obedience.

The resurrected Jesus is with us as we journey. Lent has its moments of glory as well as its hard uphill climbs. Lent has its joys and mystical experiences and intimacies with Jesus and with the community of believers as well as its penance, almsgiving, fasting, and repenting. Lent has its revelations as well as its acknowledgments of sin and the need for forgiveness. Lent has its moments of fear and the beginnings of true worship, when we see ourselves as we truly are before God, and yet stay. Lent has its inadequacies and failures, like Peter's and the others' response to Jesus' crucifixion, as well as the times when Jesus invites us to come and pray with him alone, off apart from others. Lent is for looking up and seeing only Jesus, human and with us, as well as divine and beloved of God. He shares that beloved status with us freely and generously, even as we fall on our faces, sin, and get stuck in our old ways of being, believing, and not living up to the promises of our baptism.

Transfiguration is the glory of God shining through the body of Jesus, through his flesh, his person. This glory of God is connected to us through his body: the person Jesus, eucharist, the community of believers, the church. Jesus' body is a bridge that we cross to meet God face to face. Our baptisms transfigure us individually as children of God and collectively as the body of Christ so that we can become that transfiguration, that bridge of glory, for a sinful world that needs to see God face to face.

Eventually evil and those who align themselves with evil take Jesus into their hands and seek to destroy him, to kill hope incarnate. We will need to rely on this vision of transfiguration and tell the story again and again to each other in the times ahead. In the weeks to come we will be asked to side with Jesus and so go to the cross or to stand aside and refuse, standing instead with Satan the hinderer. There are only two choices: the cross or a life that has no glory, no hope, no meaning, no future of redemption, no possibility, and no redeeming grace.

Jesus is the Light for all of us. We are to be light for the catechumens just as Jesus was light for his friends Peter,

James, and John. Today is about proclaiming the glory of God in spite of the suffering that will precede it The glory will be there. The cross too will be there. Both are reality. We have to face the challenge squarely. We must struggle to be true, to disappear so that the presence of God can be revealed, so that history can be altered to accommodate the nearness of God in our flesh and blood.

There is a children's story from the traditions of the Lenape Indian Nation, which was originally from the Pennsylvania area. It is called "Rainbow Crow," and it is a story of transfiguration that mirrors much of today's gospel.[1]

✛ Once upon a time, long ago, before any two-leggeds walked this earth, earth was at peace. It was warm, summer always, and the animals wanted for nothing. They roamed the earth and blessed the Great Spirit. Then one night, as some slept and others came out to play and hunt, there was a new thing. Things began to fall from the sky. They had seen rain before, but this was different. It was lovely, soft, very cold, and it didn't immediately disappear into the ground like rain. It stuck to the ground, to trees, branches, even fur and feathers. It stayed, growing harder and colder as it lingered. But it was lovely too. And so, when the first snowfall came, the animals were delighted that the Great Spirit was still making such grand things for earth's pleasures and needs.

But it kept snowing, long after the first night and the next day. It didn't stop, and the smaller creatures had great trouble getting around. They were trapped in their burrows, disappearing under the drifts, and exhausted from the daily need to find food. First Mouse disappeared; only a tail stuck up out of the snow. Then Rabbit and Possum and Fox. Even Coyote, sly and wily, was panting with exertion and grumpy. He was much too tired to play tricks on the others.

Some of the animals, though, were having a grand time. Otter and Seal loved the cold and snow, but even-

---

[1] This is my adaptation of the legend. A version for young readers has also been published by Nancy Van Laan.

tually they had trouble diving under the ice to get home. Moose and Elk, and even Bear, began to wonder how they'd keep their young ones strong and how long this would last. One never knew with the Great Spirit.

One day they all gathered in a rocky clearing in the forest to talk about the weather and what could be done. They quickly decided that someone had to visit the Great Spirit, to inform the Great One what was happening on earth, and ask for the snow to cease. But who was to go? Some suggested Owl, but he had trouble seeing in the light and the sun seemed so glaring with the snow on the ground. (Amazingly it snowed in darkness, with gray, thick clouds, and in bright, shining day.) Others thought of Raccoon, but he was always scavenging for food and forgetful of important things. Even Coyote was put forward, but it was pretty clear most didn't think that was wise. Coyote was a thief, a trickster—it was his nature and no one was sure exactly what he'd do on a journey to the Great Spirit, and they had enough trouble to deal with already. They were stymied. They made a terrible racket as they wailed and worried about what to do. In the meantime, the snow kept on, steady and sure, getting deeper all the time. Finally, the animals resorted to standing on top of each other in silly looking and very uncomfortable pyramids, with the largest animals on the bottom, others on top of them, and the tiniest animals at the very top. This was getting ridiculous and dangerous. How long could they keep this up?

Then from high in the pine trees came the sound of Rainbow Crow, the most beautiful of all the birds. Crow sang out: "I'll go. I'll stop the snow." And in gratitude the animals sang a song of praise and thanksgiving. Off went Crow, up and up, above the clouds and falling snow, past the winds and stars, disappearing into the darkness beyond night. Finally Crow flew right into the presence of the Great Spirit, singing and crying of the animals' plight down on earth. He sang a prayer of praise of the Creator and Maker of all things: of birds and animals, earth itself and weather, things of water and small flowers, and of the wonders that never cease, even new ones. And then the song of praise, the psalm, turned into a lullaby for the Great Spirit. Crow knew how much all the birds and animals loved to be sung to sleep and lulled by music, and since the Great Spirit made them all, why, maybe the Great Spirit would like to be sung to also! The Great Spirit listened attentively to Crow's song.

The Great Spirit delighted in Crow's lullaby, and in response Crow was told to choose any gift. Immediately Crow asked the Great Spirit to stop the snow down on earth, because all the animals and birds were disappearing under it, lost and cold. But surprisingly, the Great Spirit refused, saying, "I can't!" This surprised Crow. After all, this was the Great Spirit. Then the Great Spirit explained that Snow had a spirit and power of its own, and whenever Snow went to visit with his friend the Wind, then the snow would stop down below. But as long as Snow stayed with the Clouds, snow would continue unabated. Even when the snow stopped, there would still be cold.

So Crow asked the Great Spirit to stop the cold. Again, Great Spirit said: "I can't. I'm sorry. But I can give you another gift—the gift of Fire. It's another new thing, and it will keep you warm and melt the snow. It's very useful, a balance to Cold." And so the Great Spirit picked up a stick, put fire on the end of it, handed it to Crow, and told Crow to fly as fast as possible back down to earth. Off Crow went as fast as wings could fly, for the Great Spirit had said that the gift could only be given once. Crow had been commanded: "Go. Fly to earth before Fire disappears altogether."

Down Crow went. On the first night there were showering sparks that sprayed out as he flew fast and furious, and they darkened his tail feathers. The next day the fire crept down the stick, getting closer to Crow. It grew hotter as it ate the stick, and poor Crow was blanketed with soot as thick as the snow down below. That night the stick was a stub, and the smoke choked Crow, filling his lungs and making him cough and gag. Finally, with morning, Crow flew into the gathering, but there were no animals left to greet him on his return. They'd all disappeared under the snow! Only the highest tops of the tallest trees, very thin and sticking up like blades of grass out of the mounds of snow, remained.

Crow landed on the snow, his feet moving numbly in circles, and his voice hoarse with the cold. And soon, at first very slowly, the snow began to melt. Then it melted faster and faster. Air fed the fire; Wind stirred it up. It became Grandfather Fire, sure and hot, a beacon of hope. Finally, Crow was once again standing on firm ground, and all the animals and birds danced in a circle and sang praises of gratitude to him for saving them. But their song also sang of loss and change, for now beautiful Rainbow Crow, who once had carried all the colors in his feathers and wings, was black as a night without a moon.

When the rejoicing was over, Crow was left alone. Off he flew to his old soggy wet nest high in the pines, and he wept. He was cold and ugly. His feathers were soaked and thick, and he shook in the cold and the wind. And when he tried to sing, to soothe himself with the lullabies of old, all that came out was this terrible "caw caw caw."

Next morning Snow must have gone to visit his friend Wind, because it stopped snowing. But it was crisp and bitter cold. And still Crow cried. Finally, his cawing was noticed even by the Great Spirit, who came down in pity to hear and see what happened to poor, forlorn Crow. Great Spirit told Crow: "Soon there will be others upon the earth—two-legged creatures, very different from all the birds and animals. They will claim Fire for their own, take and use its power. In fact, they will have power over all the birds of the air and fishes of the sea and all animals—all except you, dear Crow. Because you were kind and gave me your gift of song, singing lullabies to me, and because you were so unselfish in asking for Snow to stop, no two-legged will ever have dominion over you! They won't think you're that important because you don't sing—you croak and caw and jar their ears. They won't think of eating you because your flesh is raw and sinewy and tough, like charred meat. You'd taste like smoke and ashes to them and remind them of fire's touch and destruction. And they won't even want your feathers that are as black as night and as common. But there will be a few who see clearly, as I do, and, at certain angles in the light of day or the sheen of the moon they will see the rainbows hidden in the commonness. But they'll have to get close and care and look at you kindly; others will be blind to the loveliness you carry with you always."

Crow looked, and as the sun glinted across his eyes the rainbows came and went, and he was content with the Great Spirit's blessing. The Great Spirit knew and some of the two-leggeds, the ones who saw as the Creator and Maker of all things did, would know too. And so Crow returned to his friends and crowed—"caw caw caw"—night and day, afraid of no one, not even the two-leggeds to come. He sang loudly, proclaiming rainbows that cry out concern for friends who disappear in the snow, great and small alike. And even though the two-leggeds stole fire for themselves, it is Crow who really knows fire and what it does. They say it is so to this day.

Listen to Crow's voice. It interrupts. It's insistent, loud, jarring, never-ending. There are so many of them, as black as night, as rude and bold as they can be. But they know. Listen and learn of the Great Spirit's gifts to those beloved and most like the Great Spirit who gives, never takes back, and has always something hidden away that saves the day. Caw. Caw. Caw.

The gospel is direct: "Listen to him, to the beloved of God, Jesus, only Jesus." There is a song that is good for this season of Lent, called "In the Land There Is a Hunger." It goes:

In the land there is a hunger
In the land there is a need
Not for the taste of water.
Not for the taste of bread.
In the land there is a hunger
In the land there is a need
For the sound of the word of God
upon ev'ry word we feed. (Refrain)

Hear, O Lord, my cry.
Day and night I call
My soul is thirsting for you, my God.

Your word, O Lord, is spirit and life.
You have the words, Lord of everlasting life.

Sunday of the Third Week of Lent

Exodus 17:3-7
Romans 5:1-2, 5-8
John 4:5-42

Today is a day for remembering the absolute necessity for water in our lives. Many of us in first-world countries take for granted the blessing of water. However the majority of the world still lives or dies depending on the presence or absence of water, and the well is the center of many people's lives. It is the central economic, physical, sociological, and religious reality for them—more precious than gold. Water is life itself.

The reading from Exodus begins with awareness of the lack of water: The people "in their thirst for water, grumbled against Moses, saying, 'Why did you ever make us leave Egypt? Was it just to have us die here of thirst with our children and our livestock?' The people grow bitter and test Moses and God, saying: 'Is the Lord in our midst or not?'" Water is essential for survival, both as human beings and as people belonging to God. The rock of Horeb, where God will be standing when Moses strikes it with his staff of power, will let loose a torrent of water, a flowing stream where all the people can drink and know that God is with them. We too need living waters flowing from the Rock to live with grace and truth as people of God.

The psalm refrain is pointed: "If today you hear his voice, harden not your hearts" (Psalm 95:1-2, 6-9). We are reminded not to act like our ancestors in faith, who in the face of hardship want to go back to Egypt. They complain like spoiled children even after God has called them forth into freedom, providing them with food in the desert, leading them out of slavery and into the hope of a land with peace and justice. We are not to revert to being stubborn and hardhearted, turning away from God at the first sign of trouble in our lives.

Paul's letter to the Romans tells us we have been justified by faith, and we are at peace with God through our Lord Jesus Christ. We stand in grace, hope, and glory; we can boast of this place we dwell in together, for God will not leave us disappointed. Even while we were still sinners, Christ died for us! God deals with us not justly but with an extravagant love that we must learn to trust.

The story of Jesus and the Samaritan woman at the well is a theological conversation that details her conversion and her discipleship. While she is in the town proclaiming the good news the disciples return and Jesus confesses what sustains him: the will of God, the waters of his own Spirit leaping up inside him. The waters of the Spirit are poured into our souls too, and we worship God by drawing others to Jesus.

The woman at the well models for all disciples what must happen to us again and again: we must be faced with the truth during an encounter with Jesus and the Spirit, confess our sinfulness, come to a fuller awareness of who Jesus is and so who God truly is. Then we must acknowledge who Jesus is and leave our water jar at the well, now that we have the fountain of life leaping up within us, and return to our homes and confess who we are—sinners and believers in Jesus—and convert our neighbors by telling them the good news of Jesus.

Jesus challenges the disciples and the woman in the same way—opening with a theological statement to make them think. (The woman seems to do much better with Jesus on a theological and wisdom level than the disciples do. They are a bit slow.) With the woman it is water; with the disciples it is food. Jesus' food is his work. Now the woman sets about the same work after meeting Jesus. Jesus wants the disciples to look and see, as the woman has learned to look and see. The fields ripe for the harvest are the work of the Spirit. The disciples are called to reap the firstfruits of the Spirit's labor. The villagers who heard the woman's testimony believe first because of her faith and the conversion of her life, but then they go deeper into Jesus, hearing his words and seeing the truth of his person, and they themselves continue the process of harvesting what has been sown by the Spirit. This is the story of the church community, making new believers by the power of the Spirit, the witness of believers, and the conversion of all to a deeper immersion in the waters of life, baptism. It is about initiation into the life of the Spirit.

Today's gospel and the gospels for the next two Sundays will follow a pattern: the individual's growing awareness of who Jesus is and what baptism and belief in Jesus will entail. In each story the entire process of Christian life is revealed. In today's gospel we see the Samaritan woman go from a stranger/enemy to belief in Jesus to a proclaimer of the gospel herself.

John's gospel deals with symbols, large issues, and community beliefs. Most of the individuals are meant to portray the believing community. What happens to the Samaritan woman is what has happened to us and is happening to the catechumens in this season of Lent. We are sinners who encounter Jesus, receive the gift of baptism and the waters of the Spirit springing up within us, and as disciples go back to our own places. We leave our old ways of life behind and together listen to the Word of the Lord and then obey the command to go into the fields and reap the harvest the Spirit has sown in the world. Our own small individual conversions and beliefs, our own small portions of the wisdom and understanding of the Spirit, become powerful when shared with others. Jesus is always more than we know or have experienced. He is savior of the world, and still he is more. In community and in conversion we learn to drink deeper of the Spirit.

This reading can be seen as an examination of conscience for individuals within the community of believers. We can see where we stand in the process of belief, who we think Jesus is, and what we need to do to grow to the next level of understanding and practice of our faith. This next step for all of us is given by the power of the Spirit in the Word, the scriptures, the sacraments, the liturgy, and the community itself. So, as we read the text, we can ask ourselves and our community these questions: With whom have you been at odds? Have you ever thought of Jesus coming to you through your enemy and asking for something basic from you, like a drink of water, or another necessity of life? Have you ever thought that daily encounters with strangers are openings for the Spirit of God to come to you? Who has brought you to recognize the gift of God?

Jesus tells the woman to go and get her husband, and she replies that she has no husband. Jesus tells her she is a sinner, and she accepts that reality.

When a person tells you the truth—that you're a sinner and not what you claim to be or appear to be—what is your reaction? Are you like the woman who acknowledges the truth humbly and so opens the door to change and revelation? Do you see the one who confronts you as a gift of God?

It is not until we admit that we are sinners that we can listen and learn what authentic worship is. The reality of sin gets in the way of worship. We need others and the Spirit to teach us to worship truly. How do we as a community react to our prophets and to the larger church that call us to look at our reluctance to be truthful about our relationships in the world?

Jesus also challenged the disciples. Who has challenged you, corrected you, or changed your idea and practice of authentic worship? When? The quality and extent of our worship changes and matures with the depth and quality of our conversions and confessions.

What constitutes sin for our community? What gods do we worship even as we worship the one true God: materialism, individualism, selfishness, anger, hate, nationalism, self-righteousness, pride, avarice, sloth, contemptuousness, accommodating the world, violence, insensitivity, rote worship?

The woman returns and tells what has happened to her. What kind of word of testimony do you give others so that they come to believe in Jesus? Have you ever told anyone: "He told me everything I ever did—told me I was a sinner and still accepted me, gave me water and entrusted me with his message and work, shared his Father's will with me?"

If there are catechumens in the church today, this is the day they receive the Creed, the key to faith in the community of believers. The prayer that is spoken prior to the recitation of the Creed draws much of this together for all of us:

> Lord, we pray to you for these your children, who have now accepted for themselves the loving purpose and the mysteries that you revealed in the life of your Son. As they profess with their lips their belief may they have faith in their hearts and accomplish your will in their lives. We ask this through Christ our Lord. Amen.

This is a day to emphasize the Creed—the speaking aloud the core of our faith and testifying to what we are going to stake our lives on together. These are the words, the wisdom of the Spirit, that we stand on; the Creed is our foundation and source. We are believers that Jesus Christ is the Savior of the world and that we live to draw others to the living water that springs up now in us if we are converted from our sin to the will of God.

There is a story called "Nobiah's Well," a modern African folktale written by Donna W. Guthrie. It is a deceptively simple story of a mother and her children in a village without water. The land has known drought for many years, and the daily task of going to the far-off well to get water and carry it back in a jug on the head is the central work of the entire day for village women. The water is for drinking, cooking, washing, and cleaning, but especially for watering the seeds of the small garden that feeds them. In the story the young son, Nobiah, tends the garden, hoeing and caring for the plants, watching his mother's and the other women's long daily walk and recognizing the preciousness of the water that is their lifeline and survival. This is an adaptation of Guthrie's story:

✝ One day Nobiah's mother is sick and cannot go to the well, so Nobiah is entrusted with the task—a heavy responsibility and an honor. He has become an adult. So he sets off. He walks to the well, appreciating his mother's daily labor, and he waits in line a long time for his turn at the well. Finally he fills his jug and sets off home, thirsty almost immediately. But he does not drink, for they need the water at home: his mother and sisters and the garden patch. It is hot. The sun bakes him, and the sand on his feet burns. He meets creatures along his journey home. First he meets a hedgehog who is very thirsty and pleads for water. Nobiah is kind, and he digs a small hole out with his bare hands and puts a little water in it. The hedgehog drinks it thirstily before it seeps into the sand. The hedgehog goes his way quickly and Nobiah continues his journey, the jug a bit lighter.

Next Nobiah meets a hyena with her cubs. The mother hyena begs for water, and Nobiah thinks of his baby sister. Again he digs a small hole and fills it, and they drink greedily and run off. Nobiah goes on. But again he is met by another creature, a small ant-bear. Used to the cool of the night, he is parched and near death in the noonday sun. This time Nobiah pours the water into his hands, and the ant-bear drinks from the cup of his hands. The small creature is grateful and he speaks: "Thank you, my friend. Your heart is as big and deep as the well that gives this water." Then he lopes off. By this time Nobiah is almost home.

First, he gives his baby sister a drink, then his mother. His mother tells him to take a good drink and then pour the rest of the jug on the garden; it is late in the day and the plants are wilting and in desperate need of water. He takes only a sip, but when he goes to empty the jug there are only a few drops left. His mother is frantic and yells at him—"What have you done?" Meekly Nobiah tells her that he shared his water with the small animals that he met on the way home. She cries in frustration and anger, grabs the jug out of his hands, throws it on the ground, shattering it, and collapses weeping. They have had so little water this day, and the plants are scorched, and she is still sick and unable to go to the well for the water. She scolds him: "How could you have wasted our precious water on those creatures?" Nobiah stands with his head bowed and speaks quietly: "They were as thirsty as all of us are."

It is soon night, and they all go to bed. Nobiah hears his little sister whimpering in her thirst and his mother crying as she tries to sleep and worries about the water and how they are to live tomorrow.

Finally Nobiah falls asleep, but is awakened by a noise, a scratching near his head. It is the hedgehog, calling out: "Nobiah, I am thirsty. Give me something to drink." Nobiah cries softly: "I can't. The jug is broken and there is no water." There is silence for a moment, and then the hedgehog says, "Well, then, dig a well." But Nobiah is so tired that he goes right back to sleep.

The silence doesn't last long before the scratching comes again. This time it is the hyena and her cubs, pleading for another drink. "Go away. I don't have any more water," Nobiah cries, the tears wetting his cheeks. "Well, then, dig a well for us all," says the hyena. But Nobiah is just a little boy and very tired, and he turns over and falls asleep again.

Almost immediately there is more scratching. This time it is the ant-bear, very thirsty, his tongue licking Nobiah's cheeks and tasting the salt tears. Nobiah pushes him away, grumbling that there is no water. He doesn't have any left to give. And the ant-bear too says, "Then dig a well."

This time Nobiah sits up and complains, "How can I dig a well? The sand is deep, the ground is hard, and I have just my hands."

"We'll help," comes the chorus of voices, and they all begin. The ant-bear claws, the hyenas scratch, and the hedgehog burrows. Soon Nobiah is helping. He picks up a shard from the broken pot and digs along with them. He rests often and then carries away the dirt and sand. They dig and dig and dig, but there is only sand and grit.

Nobiah asks: "How deep do we have to go?"

And the ant-bear answers, "As deep as your heart and as wide as your thirst."

But Nobiah is a small boy, and finally he lays down to rest, his head on the ground, and he sleeps long and deep. His friends keep on with the work all night.

The sun is high in the sky when Nobiah wakes up. But the first sound he hears in the morning light is the gurgle of water! He goes to the hole they all had worked on during the night and sees that there is water. Beside the hole is a new jug, with strange markings on it. Nobiah lowers the jar into the deep hole and slowly the jar fills with fresh, clear, cold water. He cries out, waking his little sister and mother, and they come running. Soon they are all screaming in delight and wonder, and all the villagers come running. "Look!" Nobiah's mother cries out, "We have our own well! We do not have to go to the far off one now." They rejoice, for now the water is with them. They will be able to quench their thirst and feed their fields.

Nobiah reminds them to share the water with the animals, who are just as thirsty and who gave him the idea for the well and worked so hard to make the gift that they now all share. And so the villagers include the animals and leave water for them. And they take the clay pot and leave it by the well, a symbol to help them remember this truth that Nobiah learned in his giving: When digging a well it must be deep as your heart and as wide as your thirst.

This third Sunday of Lent we come to the well and are reminded of the fountain of water springing up in our midst— the Spirit of God given to us in baptism. We too are asked, How deep is your heart and how wide is your thirst? We gather together around the wellspring and share the source of life: the word and the eucharist. Today we are called to dig into our souls and hearts and let ourselves be seen, sinners and yet disciples, called to salvation and rejoicing. We leave our jugs at the well and return to our places, trusting in the presence of God in our midst. We thirst for the will of God to be done on earth, for the kingdom of peace and justice to come to our towns and villages, and for God to be worshiped in our lives so that the glory of God seeps out into the world, a world that watches to see if we are truly believers in this Jesus, whose heart is deeper and wider than ever we could have hoped.

Sunday of the Fourth Week of Lent

1 Samuel 16:1, 6-7, 10-13
Ephesians 5:8-14
John 9:1-41

In the first reading the Lord sends Samuel to find the next king of Israel among the sons of Jesse of Bethlehem. The Lord tells him not to judge from appearances. God does not see as humans do, but rather looks into the heart. This line foreshadows all that is to come, not only the choice of David the shepherd as king, but in Jesus, the crucified and rejected One.

David is brought from the fields and is anointed in the midst of his brothers. From that day on, the Spirit of the Lord rushed upon David. Within the context of God's history there are individuals chosen to serve and obey God and to attend to God's interests in human history. David is one of these people. But he is a faint shadow of the One to come, the One who is the Shepherd of his people, Israel. This image of Jesus as the Good Shepherd is a foundational image of what a believer must come to see in Jesus, the prophet, the disturber of Israel, the teacher, and the One who opens the eyes of the blind to the revelation of God and to the realities of human history.

The responsorial psalm is Psalm 23, with the refrain: "The Lord is my shepherd, there is nothing I shall want." The psalm radiates the faithful sense of belonging to God in the midst of evil, sin, and opposition, of being given a place to dwell secure in the house and the pastures of the Lord—in God's community of Trinity and with the companionship of disciples in the church. It is the prayer of hope given individually to each of the catechumens, who will be taught the gospel story of the man born blind, and to all of us, who together belong only to God from the moment of our baptism.

The section of Paul's letter to the Ephesians reminds the community of our roots. We once were darkness, but now we are light in the Lord, and we are to produce every kind of goodness born of that light: justice and truth, correct judgment, and the courage to condemn the deeds of darkness. The last line

> "Awake, O sleeper,
>   arise from the dead,
>   and Christ will give you light"

is addressed to us all. Once we slept unaware of God's presence in the world, oblivious of the power of the Spirit in the Word-made-Flesh, but in our baptism we were awakened to resurrection life. Now we stand attentive and alert, summoned to bring to light what is good and expose what is evil by the light that is Christ. By our baptism "we live now no longer for ourselves alone, but we live hidden with Christ in God," and the work of Christ on earth is entrusted to us. On this fourth Sunday of Lent we will be put in the position of choosing, like the blind man given sight, whether we walk in darkness and contribute to the sin of the world or stand with Christ and against the powers that seek to destroy life.

This long story is not just about the man born blind, who comes to a deeper awareness of who healed him, who Jesus really is, and what association with Jesus will entail. It is also the story of every believer who responds to God's choosing, the outline of each of our lives as ones who have been forgiven, healed, and given the light of Christ in baptism. And it is also the story of the disciples' blindness, our continuing unawareness of the depth of our call in baptism and our slow, slow growth in the Spirit, in coming to understand who Jesus is and what it means to be his follower. Finally, it is also the story of those who choose to reject, to persecute, to destroy Jesus and all who belong to God in Christ.

This healing story is about seeing and blindness, about good and evil, and about the choices we all make—connected to our baptism and inclusion into the community that lives by the Light. We are called to reveal justice and truth to the world, and we are called also to live with the consequences of making the reality of good and evil known: suffering; rejection by our families, friends, neighbors, leaders, and the world; persecution that is personally directed at us because of our association with Jesus and our proclaimed public belief; and finally death. The week of the cross looms closer with each day of Lent.

Perhaps we should begin with a story. I do not remember where I first heard it, but it troubled me at first, so much that I couldn't tell it. Then it intrigued me, and now it has become a story that I tell again and again, learning from it each time and learning still more from the reactions it engenders in those who listen and hear, who seek to see the story in their minds and hearts. It is a Japanese story about a man born blind.

✢ Once upon a time there was a man who was born blind. He had never known anything else, and so it was part of his nature, incorporated into everything he learned: talking, walking, relations with others, and acquiring the knowledge and skills necessary for life. His blindness did not really bother him, and he made a point of not letting it stop him from doing anything that he wanted to do.

And as he grew older, he grew surer of himself. His house was arranged so that he knew where each piece of furniture and utensil was placed and he got around easily. With time, he knew each street in his village and the paths and places within walking distance: the market, side streets, the temple, and the roads out of town into the forest and fields. He had even mastered traveling to the surrounding villages, knowing the paths over the mountain and back to his own home. His senses were more acute than most, and he felt his way along, using what he smelled, heard, touched, and just sensed as he moved. Being blind didn't bother him as much as it seemed to annoy others or make others uncomfortable.

One day he traveled over the mountain to visit friends on the outskirts of another village. He had been there before; the way was easy and uneventful. The gathering with his friends and others that he met for the first time was one of the best he could remember in a long while. They feasted and talked, sang and told stories, drank and enjoyed each other's company immensely. And slowly, in twos and threes or alone, each headed for home. He was the last to leave. As he lingered at the door of his friend's house to say his thanks and goodbyes and good wishes, his host urged him to take a lantern on his way home since it had grown very dark and there was no moon out. The blind man laughed at his long-time friend. Had he forgotten that the darkness didn't concern him? He would find his way home just fine. There was an awkward silence, and then his host spoke again: "My friend, it wasn't you I was concerned about. The lantern is so that others who do not see well in the dark and are not used to being blind might know you on the path and not stumble into you or be startled or frightened."

The blind man had never thought of anyone else needing his light before and so, humbly, he took the lantern from his friend and headed over the mountain. He cleared the top of the rise and headed down, feeling his way along as he did and savoring the memories of the day and all that they had talked about and shared together, rejoicing in such good company.

And then, all of a sudden someone slammed head on into him, throwing him off the path and sending his lantern flying off away from his grasp. As he groped his way to the path, getting back on his feet again, he spoke into the darkness at the other person. "What is wrong with you? Are you blind? Did you not see my light?"

There was an awkward silence for a moment, and the voice came back: "Forgive me, friend. I saw no lantern. Your light must have gone out."

And so each went his way, the light left lost by the path. It is said that both went home blind.

The story is a parable, like many that Jesus told. Also, like many in the Zen koan tradition, it leaves us bewildered, wondering, and left with fragments of something that intrigues us and disturbs us. It unsettles us as much as being thrown off the path. Many aspects disturb us: the thought that the blind man is used to the darkness and not bothered by his lack or his loss; that he never thought that his ease in the darkness might be a danger to others; or, worse still, that his light had gone out and he was totally unaware of it. The gift given by another more aware was lost. And there is that final line: "It is said that both went home blind." There are, it seems, levels of blindness. We will let the story set and return to the story of the man born blind in John's gospel, a story that deepens the awareness of who Jesus is that was begun in the story of the woman at the well.

There are connections to today's other readings as well. David is God's chosen one, and the Spirit rushed upon him. Jesus is God's chosen one, and the Spirit of God has rushed upon him in fullness. We, by baptism, are chosen by God, and the Spirit rushes upon us and opens our eyes to begin to see as God sees. The man born blind is washed, healed, and given sight, and the Spirit rushes upon him.

What follows is a journey that continues to be revealed if we make a commitment to Jesus' person and the will of God. We are already the children of light; we are to see what others do not see in their blindness. But we are also sinners in constant need of God's healing, vision, and conversion to deeper faith and courage. We are presented with a choice. We can be blind in our sin like the Pharisees and scribes, the people who knew the man born blind and who stand around waiting to see what will happen; or we can be healed and given sight, insight, faith, the presence and knowledge of God. If we choose to see, we may be cast out of our old community, as the man born blind is, because he stands up for Jesus and holds fast to the gift of revelation.

John's gospel tells of traditions that do not appear any-where else, traditions that relate to the sacraments and the liturgical life of the community of believers, especially the process of how one becomes a believer.

In today's reading, Jesus calls for obedience from the man born blind. After obeying, the man can see. Then the man's changes really begin—radical changes in understanding, perception, and lifestyle. They continue until he has lost everything from the past and gained Jesus and the Spirit, hope, salvation and the sight and presence of God forever.

The story begins with a healing and an admonition to change what we think about sin and suffering and blindness—and where evil originates. The disciples and others believed that illness or any kind of suffering was a direct consequence of sin—if not the person's, then his parents' or family's. Jesus, however, boldly pointed out that this suffering was not the result of sin, but the place where God's glory could be revealed, where Jesus' work could be clearly shown. Our weaknesses and pains, sufferings and lacks are the places God desires to heal; they become possibilities that manifest the glory of God's mercy and kindness. Jesus *is* the light of the world, and he cannot bear any darkness that is unnecessary, destructive, or a cause for rejection and isolation. He must and he will bring the light no matter what the cost.

Baptism in the early church was often referred to as illumination, our becoming a light in Christ that will be followed by deeper belief and a commitment to Jesus and the cross, death, and resurrection in our life in community.

All that follows in the gospel, including the death and resurrection of Jesus, is the result of his healing and changing our concept of God, forgiveness, and how to live with and redeem suffering and evil in our midst. Revelation can and does lead to death on the cross. People too often prefer the darkness of ignorance, sin, evil, and injustice. Christians, who are the light of Christ in the world, must be aware of that reality and not ignore the effects of revealing the truth, of siding with the light and doing and being good and holy. The results can be rejection, persecution, loss of place in the world—the way of the cross.

The story of the blind man follows the pattern of other stories. First, his neighbors and the people accustomed to seeing him beg wonder if it is really him. The man assures them, "I'm the one." But they note that he's different. Then he tells his story—that the man called Jesus opened his eyes with mud and sent him to the pool. He obeyed, and now he can see. Simple truth-telling. When asked where Jesus is, he has no idea. He does not know anything except that his old life and person is gone, and he can see!

Second, the people take him to the Pharisees. They question him, and he repeats the story again, making a public confession of belief in what God has done for him in Jesus. The Pharisees respond not with wonder or awe or gratefulness for the man's sight and the power to bring light into the world, but with a theological point about the worthiness of one who can do this sort of thing (as if they ever could!). They use the Law, the sabbath command, to condemn Jesus and call him a sinner. Jesus is now in the same category as the man born blind, in their opinion. Others object, and an argument ensues. The words and actions of Jesus cause dissent and divisions among people! So now they ask the man who he thinks Jesus is. He answers, "A prophet." His faith is being deepened. He is learning about Jesus even though he still has not seen him, except with his eyes of faith!

This response does not sit well with the Pharisees, or anyone else for that matter. They begin to argue over the man involved. His family acknowledges that he is their son, who was blind from birth, but they will not take responsibility for anything else, or for him.

Meanwhile, the man sees more and more. He refuses to accept the Pharisees' assessment of Jesus as a sinner. He tells his story again and gets bolder (the Spirit is starting to work!), "I have told you once, but you would not listen to me. . . . Why do you want to hear it all over again? Do not tell me you want to become his disciple too?" Now the man is sounding like a teacher and a prophet himself, and the group accuses him of being a disciple of Jesus while they themselves are disciples of Moses. The man defends Jesus' relation to God, but he is ridiculed as "steeped in sin since birth." And he presumes to teach them?! They throw him out of the Temple bodily. Life is starting to get tough, and the man still hasn't even seen Jesus! He has just obeyed him in his need and desperate hope and budding faith.

Then Jesus hears of his expulsion and goes to him (like the lost sheep), and asks, "Do you believe in the Son of Man?" This is a major jump in belief! The Son of Man, the innocent one who silently offers his life as sacrifice to God and then judges with justice on behalf of the poor and the innocent. The man does not recognize Jesus, but he asks, "Who is he, sir, that I may believe in him?" Jesus reveals himself, and the man makes an act of belief and bows down to worship him. He has met and seen and been drawn into the light. He dwells secure now in the house of the Lord.

Jesus then announces,

> "I came into this world to divide it,
> to make the sightless see
> and the seeing blind."

The Pharisees react vehemently: What? You're calling us blind, counting us in with that man born blind, an obvious sinner known publicly? And Jesus responds:

> "If you were blind
> there would be no sin in that.
> 'But we see,' you say,
> and your sin remains."

The Pharisees refuse to look at the light, which reveals them in their sin and darkness; they steadfastly and adamantly reject the truth.

Jesus ends on a dark note: The dividing line is drawn. We are either with Jesus or against him. We either live in the light or dwell in the darkness. We are either made holy in the waters and forgiveness of baptism and live in Jesus' presence, or we are stuck in our sin, blind, refusing to worship God and accept the blind man as our brother. The way to the cross is close. The more we live in the light, the more intolerable those who serve and live in the darkness will find us. The story is a realistic assessment of how the world rejects those who stand in opposition to its evil.

We can ask a question or two of our community in light of the story. Are we the man born blind? the half-blind disciples?

the man's family? neighbors? onlookers? Pharisees? Where do we stand in relation to the light, to Jesus? Who do we think he is? Is he a healer/forgiver on an individual level? a prophet who reveals good and evil? Is the Word of God in our midst? the Messiah of justice and hope who will convert the nation? the Son of Man, judge of the nations, sacrifice and salvation of sinners? the Light of the World, who reveals the glory of God even in suffering, rejection, and death? Are we in great need of obedience, desperate enough to do what Jesus commands and let him touch us with forgiveness, conversion, and the renewal of our baptismal promises? Can we walk with him in the light, on the way of the cross, which will reveal the glory and kindness of God? At first reading the story appears to be about sin, but it is more about God's work in the world and about our rejoicing that the light reveals God's glory and shows evil for what it is.

Are we the children of light?

Who has opened our eyes to reality and to God in the most unlikely way? Where is Jesus for us? What do we have to say about him? Who excludes us because of what Jesus has done for us? Do we exclude anyone from the mercy of God because of our lack of sight/light? We have seen him speaking to us. How do we bring that presence to others? How do we produce justice, goodness, and truth—the deeds of light? Are we blind and in need of healing and forgiveness? Are we stubborn in our blindness, protesting that we see just fine and know who God is and what God is like? The prayer for the catechumens this day is for all of us:

Father of mercy, you led the blind man to the kingdom of light through the gift of faith in your Son. Free us from false values that surround us and blind us. Set us firmly in your truth as the children of light forever. Amen.

And now, let's look again at our Japanese story. Are we blind, and have we grown so accustomed to our blindness that we never think of the effect our way of life has on others? Are we a danger to others on the way? Has our light gone out without us even being aware of it? Are we ever the host in the story, who is the only one to think of others, to speak the truth, and to give the gift of light to share in the darkness? Has the light been left unattended on the path after our last collision in the darkness? Is it time to go visit our friends again? In what areas of our life is God wanting to shed light? And do we believe that our failures, sufferings, and lacks are the place that God uses to show forth the divine glory and to bring others to the light? Do we walk in the dark valley and yet fear no evil for God is at our side with rod and staff to give us courage (Psalm 23)?

In *The Cost of Discipleship* Dietrich Bonhoeffer writes:

> To endure the cross is . . . the suffering which is the fruit of an exclusive allegiance to Jesus Christ. When it comes, it is not an accident, but a necessity. . . . If our Christianity has ceased to be serious about discipleship, if we have watered down the gospel into emotional uplift which makes no costly demands . . . then we cannot help regarding the cross as an everyday calamity, as one of the trials and tribulations of life. We have forgotten that the cross means rejection and shame as well as suffering. . . . The cross means sharing the suffering of Christ to the last and the fullest. Only a man thus totally committed in discipleship can experience the meaning of the cross. The cross is laid on every Christian. . . . When Christ calls him, he bids him come and die.

The Light of the world intends to make the sightless see and the seeing blind. If we admit our blindness, then Jesus can spit and mix his saliva with dirt and smear it on the eyes of our soul and send us the Spirit to rush upon us and slowly turn us into the way of the Christian. With Jesus we can begin to make the light that shatters the darkness of the world and is hope in the midst of blind hate, violence, exclusion, and rage. We are the companions of the Light; once we were blind, but now we see.

Sunday of the Fifth Week of Lent

Ezekiel 37:12-14
Romans 8:8-11
John 11:1-45

How do we know God truly? The short reading of Ezekiel is heartening and precise: God is the one who opens graves and has us rise from them, who puts the Spirit within us and settles us upon our own land. This is the promise of the Lord from the very beginning, and God's promises are true. God is life itself, and life consists in having the Spirit of God within us. We can know we are in the presence of God when death is shattered and nothing seals up life and the Spirit: nothing!

Psalm 130 is the prayer of one in need, facing death and desperation, yet it is a prayer of confidence in the mercy of God: "With the Lord there is mercy, and fullness of redemption." There is no sin, no iniquity, that cannot be forgiven. Our place is to trust in the Lord "more than sentinels wait for the dawn." All of us must wait together for the Word of the Lord to be spoken.

These beginning readings are apt introductions to the demanding story of the raising of Lazarus from the dead and crucial to fleshing out the theological background of the resurrection. Romans reminds us that we live in the Spirit of God, for God dwells in us and we belong wholly to God. Our bodies are dead to sin and our spirits live because of justice. It is this same Spirit, which raised Jesus from the dead, that dwells within us, and we will know the fullness of that resurrection in our own bodies.

But the resurrection is *already* in our bodies, singing in our spirits, words, and lives. This is so basic, and yet many of us act as though we are barely alive. We must live in that Spirit, and not as though we were already in our tombs. What the Father did for Jesus has been done for us in baptism and is a continuing experience for all of us who live in Christ.

Like the psalmist of old, we cry out our hope. Out of the depths of sin, suffering, injustice, death, and violence we cry and trust in God for the fullness of life.

Chapter 11 of John is the midpoint and focus of John's entire gospel. Everything leads up to this chapter, and afterward everything is seen in light of the one singular statement of Jesus, who proclaims who he is and what he is about: "I am the resurrection and the life: whoever believes in me, though he should die, will come to life and whoever is alive and believes in me will never die." This is the heart of our belief. Jesus raises Lazarus from the dead publicly so that his disciples and the city can witness to the power of God, to Jesus' relationship with the Father, and what faith does for those who believe. Even death is redeemable in the person of Jesus. There is nothing that is not subject to the power of God in Jesus—not sin, violence, injustice, disbelief, evil, not death itself. All serve the God of life, resurrection, and the Spirit. What happened to Lazarus happens to us first in baptism, confirmation, and eucharist, and then happens in moments throughout all our lives in Christ, and then is fulfilled when we die and come into the resurrection along with all the world.

The long form of this reading is necessary to set up the events of Holy Week. We will all be brought back from the dead—released from the power of sin, evil, and death—and given a new life in the Spirit for all to see, one that will bring others to belief in Jesus.

The story begins strangely. Word comes to Jesus that Lazarus is sick unto death, and yet Jesus deliberately delays going to him and lets him die. Jesus announces that what happens to Lazarus, his beloved friend, is to serve God and give glory to God. The gospel states very clearly that Jesus loved Martha and her sister Mary and Lazarus. They are friends and disciples, part of the inner circle of Jesus' community. Then, after two more days, Jesus goes back to Bethany over the protests of the disciples, who know what's waiting for them in nearby Jerusalem: rejection and people who have already tried to stone him to death. They are timid and fearful and unsure. But Jesus tells them that Lazarus is asleep, and that he is going to awaken him. They misunderstand, and so he plainly tells them that Lazarus is dead. It is Thomas who says, resignedly: "Let us go along with him, to die with him." And this is the heart of what these next two weeks are about: Do we understand what we're saying and doing, or not?

They arrive at Bethany, and they hear that Lazarus has been in the tomb for four days already. The word spreads and Martha runs out to meet Jesus on the road. Many people spread the word that Jesus has returned to console Mary and Martha. Martha encounters Jesus and immediately hits him with the words: "Lord, if you had been here, my brother would never have died. Even now, I am sure that God will give you whatever you ask of him." Her address is part faith, part rebuke, part desperation, and part grief. And Jesus responds: "Your brother will rise again." Martha adds, "Yes, on the last day."

Again, we are hearing a theological conversation in the presence of grief and death, loss and mourning. This is a place of proclamation, of teaching, of leading the catechumens and the church to the place of Lazarus's tomb. No one understands the depth of Jesus' power or that Jesus is God. So Jesus announces who he is: "I am the Resurrection and the Life: whoever believes in me, though he should die, will come to life; and whoever is alive and believes in me will never die." This is the whole reason for our baptism, our promises, our commitment to God as church, as the body of Christ. This is our statement of belief, which we grow into every day of our lives and which forms the pattern of our death to sin, our burial in the waters of baptism, and our being raised to life by the Spirit even now. Jesus asks her: "Do you believe this?" (a question directed to the catechumens and to us repeatedly), and she responds with her statement of who Jesus is: Son of God, Messiah, and all that those titles represent.

Then she turns around and goes back to the house to get Mary, telling her: "The Teacher is here, asking for you." Mary encounters Jesus on the path and begins with the same line as Martha: "Lord, if you had been here my brother would not have died." A large crowd accompanies her. Jesus sees her weeping and all those with her, and he is troubled in spirit and moved by the deepest emotions. This is a description of Jesus in the face of death. He asks where Lazarus is, and they say: "Come and see." (Note that these were Jesus' first words to those who followed him and asked him who he was in the first chapter of John.) The reaction of the crowd is mixed: "See how much he loved him." Others are more cynical: "He opened the eyes of the blind. Why could he not have done something to keep him from dying?" And once again, Jesus is troubled in spirit. This description is an allusion to the power of God moving in Jesus as it moved over the water of the Red Sea and as it moves over the waters of baptism. The Spirit troubles us.

They come to the tomb, a cave with a stone across it. Jesus gives a command: Take away the stone. And Martha reacts: "It has been four days now; surely there will be a stench!" Jesus once again has to reassure her and call her again to belief. It is one thing to profess to believe, another altogether to act upon it and to integrate it into our mind and heart. Words are one thing. Staking our life on it is something else.

Martha is told that if she believes she will see the glory of God. The others obey and take away the stone. Jesus prays aloud so that everyone will know what he is doing and where his power comes from—from God who sent him to bring life and to undo death. Then he calls Lazarus forth. Lazarus hears the voice, the Word of God. And even in death, he obeys. He is bound hand and foot, wrapped for burial, and Jesus commands the disciples, "Untie him and let him go free." Lazarus is freed from sin, evil, death, from anything that holds him captive. And it is the community of believers that frees him, facing him in the direction of a new life.

Many who see what Jesus has done put their faith in him. But we know that Jesus' action must have fanned the flames of others' hatred against him. Bringing someone back from the dead—opening graves and releasing the stench—brings people to belief, conversion, and hope, and also turns people against the life of the Spirit.

Jesus' actions are rooted in his single-hearted faith in his Father and what he is in the world for—sent to bring life out of death, resurrection out of despair, loss, and sin. This is the risk and glory of incarnation, of God becoming human and sharing our mortality and his immortality, even as we live as human beings subject to death here on earth. Resurrection life begins here and grows into fullness at our death!

It seems that the closer our relationship to Jesus, the more he may demand of us—letting us suffer and die so that others might come to belief. Association with Jesus and the gift of life in resurrection and intimacy with the voice and Word of the Lord align us so closely with Jesus that people will react the same way to our presence as they do to Jesus' presence. God, who loves us dearly, will not save us from mortal death but, better, from death due to sin, injustice, and evil.

There are many personal questions that the gospel calls us to reflect upon. When did we send for the Lord and he delayed in coming to our aid? How did we feel? What happened? What was our reaction to God's timing in relationship to our need? What kind of expectation do we put on Jesus, especially in times of grief, great need, sadness and suffering? Perhaps the core question is based on Jesus' declaration to Martha: "I am the resurrection and the life: whoever believes in me, even though he should die, will come to life; and whoever is alive and believes in me will never die." *Do we believe this?* Whose death has tested our belief in the resurrection? When has it been hard for us to believe? Did we trust God at that time? Do we trust God with our life now, no matter what is happening in history and in our small part of the world?

Jon Sobrino wrote a letter to his friend Ignacio Ellacuría, who was murdered in El Salvador while Sobrino was away. Written a year after the massacre, Sobrino tries to put into words what Ellacuría's life had meant for him and what it had come to mean for him now. In part, Sobrino writes:

Ellacu, this is what you've left us, or at least left me. Your exceptional capacities could dazzle, and your limitations could confuse. I think, Ellacu, that neither the one has bedazzled me nor the other obscured what, to me, is the rock-bottom thing you've left me: that there's nothing more essential than the exercise of mercy in behalf of a crucified people, and nothing more humane and humanizing than faith. These are the things I've had in my head for years now. Today on the first anniversary of your martyrdom, I say them. With pain and with joy—but especially, with gratitude. Thanks, Ellacu. For your mercy, and for your faith.

Ignacio Ellacuría, a Jesuit, was one of my first theology teachers. It was a class on Christology, a very small class of only six people. That one semester, four months, exploded every thought and concept that I had of God. It threw me into confusion and opened places in my heart I had long ago closed. Ever since I have listened and studied in light of his questions, passion, and brilliance, his analytical and religious probing mind. When I heard the news that he had been killed by blowing out his brains, specifically because the murderers found his mind so dangerous, something in me died and I felt anger as I had never known before. Over time, with reflection, prayer, and study, he has continued to teach me, bringing some of that faithfulness and mercy that Jon Sobrino speaks about. It is his death that has most profoundly shaken my faith and caused me to ask myself, Do I believe that Jesus is the Resurrection and the Life? Do I believe that all who believe in Jesus, even though they die, will come to life again, and if they are alive that they will never die? His death has made my response less tentative, more bold. I have become more aware of the power of life and the response it can evoke in others: hatred, rage, and the burning desire to kill hope in the flesh and words of believers.

Jesus wept at the death of Lazarus. When have we seen Jesus weep? What makes God weep? What evokes the strongest emotions in Jesus? Are these the same things that evoke our emotions and reactions? Do we believe that Jesus loves us as much as he did Lazarus, Martha, and Mary? Has he wept over us in our tomb? How long have we been in our tombs—four days? Are we more afraid of the stench of opening tombs and exposing the rot in our lives and the world, than of the possibility of the Word of God calling us and others forth into life and wholeness? Where have we seen the glory of God in the midst of death? Why doesn't Jesus stop people from dying? Why doesn't God stop evil, injustice, and sin in the world?

Sometimes the deaths of those who are closest to us both test our faith and give us heart. Our belief says that Jesus stopped death in his own dying. Now our death and the deaths of those we love and cherish give glory to God in the death of Jesus Christ.

We stand with Jesus in his revulsion for death and yet with him in trust as well, as he prays to his Father for life. Jesus' prayer is ours: "Father, I thank you for having heard me. I know that you always hear me but I have said this for the sake of the crowd, that they may believe that you sent me." We believe and go through these last weeks of Lent into Holy Week saying: "If we have died to ourselves in Christ, then we shall rise to new life in him."

On this day, the catechumens are given the prayer of the Our Father. Jesus prays, and we learn how to pray by practice. In today's readings, Jesus prays by waiting, returning, by always turning everything into the glory of God, by letting others hear his own belief in his Father, by questioning Martha and calling her again to stake her actions on her words of belief, by commanding his disciples to help him in the work of bringing forth Lazarus from the tomb, loosing him and all people from that which binds us to death, violence, unnecessary pain, and evil. It is the voice of the Word of the Lord that brings Lazarus forth from the tomb, into the light. We hear that same Word daily in the scriptures and in one another's faith. We are to pray without ceasing, without losing heart, pray always so that the glory of God is revealed in us, as it was in Jesus Christ.

There is an old Jewish story about prayer that has haunted me since I first discovered it. It is one of the stories of the Baal Shem Tov, the Master of the Good Name.

✢ Once upon a time there was a good and faithful rabbi. The day of Yom Kippur came, and all day the rabbi had fasted, done penance, and prayed for his people, his small congregation. That night, the holiest night of the Jewish year, they were all gathered in the synagogue praying, asking for forgiveness and mercy from God, blessed be his Name. The rabbi stood with his back to the people, wrapped tightly in his prayer shawl, and prayed. He prayed as fervently and intensely as he could. He remembered that every synagogue around the world gathered the Jews together on this day and all their prayers were ascending to God, the Holy One.

As he prayed, he begged God for some sign that his prayer on behalf of his people was heard. As soon as he thought it and prayed it, he was taken aback. Why should the Holy One respond to such a prayer, when there were probably many others, hoping for the same thing? And yet, almost instantaneously, he was given an answer to his prayers. For just a moment he heard the voice of God, clear and ringing out like a bell: "Have Tam offer your prayers to me, and I will graciously accept all of you back into my heart, forgiving all things and showering my mercy upon you." And then, just as surely the light, the sense, the sound, was gone. The rabbi stood with his back to the people praying still, and he was alone.

Then he turned and came toward the people. Instead of praying the prayer of intercessions as the ritual demanded, he called out: "Tam! Tam! Where is Tam?" He knew what everyone was thinking—he had been thinking it himself just seconds before. Why Tam? Tam was hardly ever in the synagogue. He was poor, unlettered, and worked so hard that he often missed services. Oh, he was a good-hearted enough soul, but he certainly hadn't amounted to much in the community. The rabbi didn't even know exactly what Tam did for a living. The people were stunned, shocked.

And poor Tam, who was in fact in the synagogue on this holy night, was equally stunned. He was paralyzed and could not move. Why did the rabbi call out his name instead of praying? What terrible thing was about to be visited upon him? But others in the synagogue recognized him, and the rabbi gestured to them to carry Tam forward to the front of the synagogue. Tam stood, silent, with head bowed before the rabbi.

The rabbi spoke loudly and directly to Tam. "I have been praying for mercy and forgiveness for all of us on this night and I have been clearly told by God, blessed be his Name, that we all will be forgiven and taken back into the heart of God if you pray for us, if you give your prayer to God on our behalf."

Tam was speechless. How could he pray? He could not even read the service, the prayers in the book. But the rabbi was insistent. God would only take the community back into his heart and give them a year of blessing, grace, and mercy if Tam prayed for them. He had to pray for them! Finally, Tam agreed. But he looked at the rabbi and said: "I have to go get my prayers."

What? the rabbi thought. You have to go get your prayers? "Then go," he said.

Tam ran down the aisle, pushing people aside. Everyone was in confusion and disarray. But Tam did not live far, just down a side street away from the synagogue's back door. He was back in no time.

Once again there was tumult in the synagogue as Tam returned to the front to stand beside the rabbi and pray on behalf of the community. He stood before them all, and in his hands was a large earthen pitcher. He lifted it high, turned his back on the people, and addressed God. "O Holy One, you know I am not good at praying, but I bring you all I have. This pitcher holds my tears. Late at night, even when I am tired, I sit and try to pray to you. And then I think of my poor wife and children and the fact that they have no clean clothes to wear to services and are ashamed to come to the synagogue, and I cry. And then I think of all the hungry ones, the beggars on the steps of the synagogue and in the streets, in the cold and rain, miserable and so alone, and I cry some more. And then, God, I think of what we do to each other. I think of all the gossip and hate, all the quarrels and wars, and I think of you crying, God, of you looking down on us hurting one another so, and I know that you weep for us always. God, I cry for you and how we must break your heart and sadden you so. Please, take my tears, accept my prayers, and take all of us back into your heart once again. Give us a blessing and forgive us in your great mercy and kindness."

And Tam took his pitcher and poured his tears over the floor of the synagogue. There was a long silence, and then the rabbi spoke, haltingly: "God has heard Tam, and we are forgiven. We are once again the people of God. Let us live this year with grateful hearts."

The people sang, but they left the synagogue quietly. They vowed never to forget Tam's prayer or his pitcher of tears and to make sure there would be less to cry over in the years to come. They looked at Tam and his family differently, and their neighbors too. Some even reconciled with their enemies. But they all went home thinking of the tears of God.

Today God weeps over the death of a friend, his beloved Lazarus. Perhaps he wept too because of his disciples' faint-heartedness and lack of understanding. Or maybe he wept over Martha and Mary's chiding words: "If only you'd been here," not even allowing him to grieve and mourn his friend's suffering and death. Or did he weep at the hardness of peoples' hearts, looking for something to complain about and find fault with, no matter what he did? Did he weep at death, at sin, at evil, at injustice, and at the prospect of his own death at the hands of religious people sure of God and faith yet so disrespectful of life and human dignity? Did he weep at our lack of passion and lack of belief, ardently desiring that we might come to believe in him as the resurrection and the life?

God weeps today still. There is sin, insensitivity to the terrible destruction of other human beings, physical deaths and killings, unnecessary suffering, famine, economic injustice, and many people who do not rejoice in those who were dead being brought back to life. There are those who plot to kill anyone whose presence brings hope to those who are desperate. There is much to weep over. We, like Jesus, are sent to stand before the tombs and call one another forth with the word of God and to untie and set each other free. We are to encourage one another in faith to live the resurrection life now. We are to stake our lives on the mercy of God and the fullness of redemption, to be the beloved friend of Jesus, like Lazarus, responding to the sound of his voice, even in death. We are to live now, free, for the glory of God revealed in the body of Christ, the church today.

We pray for all those who have died. In faith, we pray:

Lord Jesus, like a shepherd who gathers the lambs to protect them from all harm, you led us to the waters of baptism and shielded us from harm. Now carry us on the path to your kingdom of light where we will find happiness and every tear shall be wiped away. To you be glory, now and forever. Amen.

And we pray for ourselves:

Lord Jesus, by raising Lazarus from the dead you showed that you came that we might have life and have it more abundantly. Through your Spirit, who gives life, fill us with faith, hope, and charity, that we may live with you always in the glory of your resurrection, for you are Lord forever and ever. Amen.

Passion/Palm Sunday

From the Procession with Palms: Matthew 21:1-11
Isaiah 50:4-7
Philippians 2:6-11
The Passion Account, Matthew 26:14-27:66

This week, all the catechumens, those who have helped to prepare them for baptism, and all those who believe in Jesus and have been baptized will be together. We set our faces with Jesus toward Jerusalem, toward the cross, death, and resurrection. This week we will be crucified in our hearts and souls, give glory to God with Jesus, and experience again our baptisms and renew our promises. We will pass over with Jesus and go through the tomb into the life born of water and the Spirit.

This is the week of telling the story again and having it come true in us and our communities. We remember especially the crucified One, a sign of scandal and hope, a sign of contradiction (1 Corinthians 1:18f.). It is time for us to experience upheaval, wrenching away from the grasp of the world, and becoming more deeply converted to our baptismal promises and the explosion of the kingdom of God into our world. This week the word and the power of the cross must become part of our flesh and bones so that the world can be injected anew with the Spirit of God.

We begin outside the church—in courtyards, plazas, parking lots, and side streets—for the procession of palms and a short reading from Matthew that sets the stage for our celebration. The rites of Holy Week are familiar to some, strange to others. They are all meant to be celebrated—participated in and absorbed into our very bloodstream and heart. The older sense of the verb *to celebrate* meant "to frequent," "to hold in regard," and that is what we are to practice these days. We are to frequent the company of and honor the Suffering Servant of God, the crucified One, and all those who today wear that mantle of pain laid on them by a world that still experiences violence, despair, and hatred as a usual way of living.

The crowd draws near to Jerusalem, entering Bethphage on the Mount of Olives. They have come to celebrate the feast of freedom, the feast of Passover, the memorial of God drawing the people out of slavery and oppression into hope and an embrace of belonging as God's people. Jesus has come to celebrate with his disciples and friends a last time, and he sends two of the disciples off with instructions to prepare for his arrival and entrance into the city. They are to take an ass that they find tethered and her colt, and if anyone tries to stop them, they are to reply: "The Master needs them." That is how he will come into the city. The prophets will be remembered and their words repeated: "Tell the daughter of Zion, Your king comes to you without display astride an ass, astride a colt, the foal of a beast of burden." Jesus stays close to the earth, close to the poor and the laborer and the slave, those made beasts of burden by the mighty and the haughty.

There are other echoes too. Abigail, for example, rode an ass into David's camp to seek forgiveness and reconciliation for her husband's crimes and to plead for his life. She came humbly, as a sign of peace, knowing that the lives of many depended on her intervention.

So, the disciples lay their cloaks on the animal, and Jesus rides into the city. The people lining the streets on the way to the feast spread their cloaks on the road, and others cut branches from the trees, laying them in his path. These are honors and signs that their hope and their lives have been offered to him. They cry out: "God save the Son of David! Blessed is he who comes in the name of the Lord! God save him from on high!" This is a portion of the Sanctus, which we cry out and sing with the angels and all of creation, acknowledging God. We serve only God, no other power on earth. For the people of Jesus' time, the words expressed a religious and heart-felt hope laced with a nationalism born of long persecution, loss of sovereignty and dignity, heavy taxation, and grinding poverty.

In last week's gospel we read that Jesus was stirred to his very soul. Now it is the city that is stirred to its depths, demanding: "Who is this?" And the answer keeps coming back: "This is the prophet Jesus from Nazareth in Galilee." The depths contain the unknown, the uncontrollable, the dangerous elements, the underside of a city, and they are demanding to know who it is that disturbs, as prophets do just by their presence. The prophet Jesus is the Savior from the north, from the place where revolution is fomented and rebels abound, a place of struggle on the boundaries of Israel. There is excitement, expectation, fear. Plots are already afoot. Jesus knows what he is walking into. His moment of triumph will be painfully short-lived. But he has come to confront Jerusalem—and to stand before each of us and invite us to choose.

We remember that beginning of the week called holy, called passion, by carrying our own palms. These palms will be burned and the ashes for next year's Ash Wednesday will be made from them. The sign of glory and the sign of conversion are made of the same stuff and meet in our flesh and lives. We walk and sing the praises of the One who goes before us. We follow together. It will be a long week for all of us.

Once back in church the first reading is proclaimed from the book of Isaiah. It is a humble description of Jesus and of all those persecuted for the sake of justice and of God's honor. "The Lord God has given me a well-trained tongue, that I might know how to speak to the weary a word that will rouse them." This is not just a word of comfort or consolation, but the rousing word of the good news, the imminent coming of the kingdom breaking into the lives of those who are bent under the weight of evil and the world's inequality and false idols. "And morning after morning he opens my ear that I may hear; And I have not rebelled, have not turned back."

This word teaches how to resist without violence or hatred, how to endure in the face of humankind's inhumanity, and how to rely on a strength that is always offered. Jesus, the Suffering Servant, and the prophets before and after him, the innocent and the just, have "not rebelled, have not turned back, but they have given their bodies to those who beat them and their faces to those who insulted and humiliated them." Their shield, which they grasped and held onto for a dearer life, was God.

"For the Lord God is my help." This is the cry of those who seek to be human rather than to kill or harm others. Even though such a one may die, ultimately there will be no disgrace. But it is hard. Jesus sets his face like flint, knowing that he will not be put to shame and knowing equally that he will be tortured and mocked, reduced to sheer brokenness by other human beings. Through all, he will cling to God. He is our model. St. Paul calls it folly and wisdom, the word and the cross. It is a two-edged sword, a healing balm and grace, a hungry lion, a hammer-shattering rock, and a source of freedom and life, especially for those who are crushed under the heel of hatred and broken by the structures of injustice.

Today is a day of processions, circuses, a band of motley followers who are, along with the holy fools of long ago, meant to keep alive the tradition and belief of the Holy Fool who was stripped naked, cursed, beaten publicly, and forced outside the city and hung on wood in a garbage dump. St. William of Thierry (1085-1148) calls this "holy madness," madness for the sake of love. This is Jesus. This is God, who is so close to the miserable and the wretched of the world: those starving in a world aplenty, those being bombed in Sarejevo, those being hacked to death by neighboring tribes in Africa, those dying slowly of cholera and tainted water and bureaucracy in South America, those on the street in every city, all those outcast from society, culture, and even religion's often narrowly defined boundaries.

Christ, this holy fool, mad with the truth, is part of the ancient tradition of the prophet and the mystic, one who atones for others and refuses to let us keep existing in systems where there is *truly* madness: insensitivity, hostility toward strangers and the poor, and fear of those who are different. The cross cries out loudly that our religion is about uncrucifying the world, about resisting unnecessary pain and humiliation, about standing with those caught in the net of nationalism and ideologies more intent on making their points rather than lifting up people, about true worship. The cross will not tolerate anyone being destroyed while believers spend time and money and effort on buildings, environments, and ways of spirituality.

This week profoundly disturbs the world and is meant to disturb us, break us out of complacency and false pieties. It shatters any sense of self-righteousness we might still entertain in our hearts or practices. God has known this all along and so came to dwell among us, among the most poor and lost of his time.

The ancient psalm with its lament, "My God, my God, why have you abandoned me?," is horrible in its litany of what human beings do to each other and allow others to experience. It is about pain and how to stay human when we fall into the hands of those who consider other lives expendable or mere commodities to be used or destroyed. It is about pain of the body, and worse, pain of the soul caused by the mockery and blasphemy of others calling on God to help us because they won't. The one who is tortured is left with nothing of the past, of material possessions, of dignity.

The only thing remaining is hope, unbridled and unreasonable hope in God: "I will proclaim your name to my brethren; in the midst of the assembly I will praise you." "You who fear the Lord, praise him; all you descendants of Jacob, give glory to him." At the end, what makes us human is the One whom we worship, whom we serve and obey, whom we praise and give glory to, even when lives are tattered or bruised or even taken from us violently. The suffering are reminded that God is not far from them, and God is their aid and help. They, like Jesus, are abandoned to the hands of God when others refuse to help them.

And so the second reading from Philippians reminds us what our attitude must be—like that of Christ. Jesus' message of the breaking in of the reign of God, his companionship with public sinners and those who did not conform to society's norms, and his forgiveness and reconciliation of all have led him to this week when Jesus "emptied himself and took the form of a slave, being born in the likeness of men. He was known to be of human estate, and it was thus that he humbled himself, obediently accepting death, even death on a cross!"

It is this emptying, this obedience, this humbling surrender, that is the source of the glory that is extended to Jesus by God, who will exalt him and bestow on him the name that saves, the name that glorifies God, the name that makes us, with Jesus, the children of God. This name thunders and reverberates in the sea, the sky, under the earth, and in all hearts as all creation proclaims and cries out: "Jesus Christ is Lord!" That is what this week of passion is about. We are called to stand with Jesus and to die with him.

This week is about standing up for our belief. If we believe in Jesus Christ, we believe in the poor and those who suffer the injustices of the world. There is no separation between the two. We must read the passion accounts and hear of the terror and destruction of what was done to God in Jesus with the same horror and dismay that we hear of what is done to others in the world today—what we do, or what we allow to be done in our name, in collusion or without our resisting the deeds.

The backdrop against which we, as believing Christians in the 1990s, must read the passion accounts is not so much the personal experience of Jesus, the prophet of Nazareth in Galilee, but the present and all those who are God's chosen ones, the suffering on the earth. The cross is as much a symbol of life as it is of death. We are marked with this sign, blessed with it, christened with it. We trace it on others' fore-heads, hands, and hopefully hearts. This emptying, this obe-dience, brings life out of the pain, injustice, hatred, and vio-lence. Jesus' pain and ours redeem the world. We have a part in this struggle and the work of the coming of the king-dom into the world.

This week of passion means passion for life, truth, God's honor, the poor, and the reign of goodness in the world. We take up our cross, as Jesus took up his cross, and we take it to the world, to the victims of injustice as a sign of hope and freedom and also to those who do evil in the world as a sign of judgment and justice. "Rejoice and be glad," we are told in Matthew. "Happy are you when people abuse you and persecute you and speak all manner of calumny against you on my account. Rejoice and be glad" (Matthew 5:11-12).

Matthew's account of Jesus' betrayal, trial, and destruc-tion is short. First, the betrayal is arranged for thirty pieces of silver. Then there is the meal, the celebration of Passover, which begins with Jesus' announcement that one of them will betray him. Judas is acknowledged. The meal contin-ues. Bread is broken and shared. Wine is blessed and shared. But Jesus does not eat and drink; he waits for the new wine in the kingdom. And they go out singing to the Mount of Olives. Jesus reminds them that their faith will be shaken, the shepherd will be struck, the sheep scattered, but after he is raised up, he will go to Galilee ahead of them. And Peter brashly boasts of his strength, and Jesus tells him that Peter will disown him before dawn.

And Jesus prays, inviting the others—especially Peter, James, and John—to pray with him. He experiences sorrow and distress, his heart nearly broken with sorrow. He falls before God and prays: "My Father, if it is possible, let this cup pass me by. Still, let it be as you would have it, not as I." Three times. And three times he comes to his friends and they are asleep. He is alone. Then Judas comes into the garden and betrays him with an embrace and kiss. There is a scuffle, fighting, and one of the servants loses an ear. Jesus' words are strong: "Put back your sword where it belongs. Those who use the sword are sooner or later destroyed by it." Jesus resists evil with every bone and fiber of his body and spirit but not with violence, only with the force of truth-telling and his presence. He is taken as a brigand, as a prophet, and he is taken alone.

At the trial with Caiaphas, the high priest, Jesus declares: "Soon you will see the Son of Man seated at the right hand of the Power and coming on the clouds of heaven." He is accused of blasphemy and sentenced to death. He is spit at, hit, and insulted as a prophet, as the Messiah, taunted and held bound. Outside, Peter is vehemently denying that he even knows him. He meets Jesus' eyes for a moment and goes to weep bitterly, disappearing from the story.

Jesus is taken to Pilate, and Judas regrets his action, trying to give back the silver. He confesses his sin but is rejected, and he hangs himself. He too disappears from the story, except as a memory. Jesus, standing before Pilate, is silent. It is the custom to release a prisoner on the feast. The choice: Barabbas, a murderer, or Jesus, the prophet of life? Even Pilate's wife has a dream about Jesus, the holy man, and she exhorts her husband to have nothing to do with his death. Even in dreams Jesus is upsetting. But the crowd cries out for the death penalty: "Crucify him." Pilate is afraid of a riot; the city is packed with people, and he cannot afford that. The crowd becomes a mob. So the responsibility is laid on the people, and Pilate washes his hands of the whole affair. Jesus is handed over to the soldiers and is publicly scourged: his flesh torn by rawhide tipped with metal. Later he is wrapped in a military cloak and crowned with thorns. He is insulted in his pain, tormented, and led to crucifixion.

One man helps Jesus, conscripted into service, a Cyrenian named Simon, who carries his cross. Then he is crucified, his clothes divided among his executioners. Above his head hang the words: "This is Jesus, King of the Jews"—a terrible follow-up to "This is Jesus, the prophet from Nazareth in Galilee." He is taunted by the crowd to show his power, to save himself. But where are his disciples, friends, followers, those whom he cured and forgave? Where are they? Where have they all disappeared to?

Jesus' words "My God, my God, why have you forsaken me?" are words of prayer. The earth reacts violently. The curtain of the Temple is torn in two from top to bottom. There is an earthquake. The soldiers are terrified, and one makes the declaration of faith that belongs to Matthew's community: "Clearly this was the Son of God!" Jesus is dead.

Many women, among them Mary Magdalene, Mary the mother of James and Joseph, and Mary the mother of James and John, come and with Joseph of Arimathea they take the body down, wrap it, and put it in the tomb. Two of the women remain, keeping watch, sitting there, facing the tomb. The tomb is secured by guards because there are some who remember his words about rising. A seal of the Roman government is placed upon the tomb. Jesus disappears into the ground.

The way of Jesus is the way of the cross, which leads to rejection, the experience of injustice, becoming a victim, and finally death. Life is the only gift we have to offer to God in worship and in compassion to one another. This week we gather it up, take it in our hands to offer it, with Jesus and the body of Christ, the church, back to the Father, praying with the power of the Spirit:

> But you, O Lord, be not far from us; O my help, hasten to aid us. We will proclaim your name to our brothers and sisters; in the midst of the assembly we will praise you: You who fear the Lord, praise him; all you descendants of Jesus Christ, give glory to God.

Our attitude must be that of Christ. This week we learn how to empty ourselves as we listen to and tell the story of Jesus. It is a dangerous story, full of risk and resurrection, for those who believe.

CYCLE B

Christ Emmanuel Flowering Cross

Introduction

The readings for cycle B use the most ancient stories of the Bible to remind us of the primary symbols and initial promises of God that herald the coming among us of Jesus, the Son of Man, the crucified One. The gospel readings for the first two Sundays are alternate accounts of the testing in the desert and the transfiguration, this time from Matthew and Mark respectively. They focus closely on the cross and persecution, on suffering for our belief and for belonging to Jesus.

The first readings from Genesis show how God has been saving us since the beginning. First, there is the story of Noah and God's promise that never again will water be the source of death. This hints, of course, that water instead will be the source of everlasting hope and life. Next is the story of Abraham and the binding of Isaac, with the final word that God does not desire the life of a person as sacrifice. God wants the hearts and wills of the chosen people.

The second readings from the pastoral letters reinforce and flesh out what these stories mean for believers today. In cycle B the second readings are to the point; they act as reminders of the theology and statements of faith that are told in story form in the readings.

The final three Sundays continue the original pattern. We look at history expanding as God claims the Israelite people in the desert and gives the Law as testament to their relationship. We are to be faithful as God is faithful. Paul's exhortation revolves around the crucified One as the ultimate reality of faithfulness. The gospel from the second chapter of John slams home the connections between life and worship, between integrity within the community and liturgy. There is to be no separation of what we do in church and what we do in the world. We are to live with zeal for the house of the Lord; the kingdom of God is to be our first allegiance.

These readings, just prior to Holy Week, are demanding, confrontational, and aggressive. They insist that we be truthful in all areas of our lives.

Next we hear the shameful litany of infidelity, dishonesty, and every form of evil contrasted with God's enduring patience and grace. God sends the prophets to us and seeks only that we return with hearts broken and open to God's word. This chronicle of grief and hope reiterates that God has loved us from the first and loves us to death, even unto the death of his beloved Son, the Christ, whom we are to follow in grace.

Then we hear John's account of Nicodemus, who comes in the dark to sit in the presence of the Light of the world. Nicodemus learns to look upon the crucified One and to look as well at what evil does to human beings. We can choose to be delivered from death, as those in the desert were delivered by looking upon the serpent that had stung them.

Last we hear the prophet Jeremiah's call to know the Lord. The heartening promise of a new covenant of flesh and blood is planted in our hearts to draw us more deeply than ever into the heart of God through forgiveness. The reading from Hebrews tells us about that covenant where we, like Jesus, are to learn obedience in the midst of suffering, to reverence God in all times and seasons, and to pray unceasingly. Then John's account of Jesus' sermon on the grain of wheat that must fall into the ground in order to bring forth fruit drives home our understanding of the relationship among suffering, death, and resurrection. This is the hour for which Jesus was born, the hour of passion that is the beginning of resurrection.

Now we are ready for Holy Week, for being formed in the likeness of Christ crucified, obedient and reverent before God in the face of inhumanity, sin, evil, and injustice on the earth. Now the sentence is passed on the world. We are judged, and we have only two options: to stand with Jesus, the servant of the Father, or to stand with evil in opposition to the will of God.

This cycle can be summed up in a nutshell: Don't just stand there, do something. These readings are steeped in faithfulness—the reality of God's enduring grace and presence in our lives and in the history of the world, intent on saving us. This is contrasted with our sad lack of faithfulness and our weakness. Who are we? Can the world tell that we are the people of God, intent on true worship and being a light to the nations? Or are we like so many who have gone before us in faith, straying and intent on doing evil and resisting the coming of God among us? We are called to choose where we stand.

Sunday of the First Week of Lent

Genesis 9:8-15
1 Peter 3:18-22
Mark 1:12-15

It is Lent again, the season of being seen, seen through, and called to account for our baptisms and life. Each year the church admonishes us to turn our faces once again to the mystery at the heart of our faith: the paschal mystery of the living, dying, and rising of Jesus and our own living, dying, and rising with Jesus. This cycle of readings, which concentrates primarily on the gospel of Mark, is often playfully and ruefully referred to as the "killer B" readings because of their intensity. They insist that we radically alter our lives as individuals who claim to believe in Jesus as Lord and as the community that mirrors that belief to a world often intent on ignoring or destroying hope and freedom.

The readings go back to roots that we tend to forget—our source for hope and also for our weaknesses. But they also contain the rich symbols of God's presence among us since the beginning, seeping through history and trying to get our attention again and again as we wander about, seeking our own ways rather than the way of God in the world. We go back to see where we went off track and left the hope and intention of God's original plan of life and growth in balance and harmony. We go back to the story of Noah, a "*re*-creation" story, a step in putting things back together after they have begun to unravel. A covenant is established between Noah and his sons and daughters, his descendants and our ancestors in faith. But it is also established with all living creatures, with everything wild and tame that was saved in the ark.

The covenant is constituted by a promise: the earth will not be destroyed again by flood or waters. The sign of this covenant is the bow that appears in the clouds; the rainbow, the arc/ark of the covenant that lingers in the sky, reminds all of the presence and kindness of God and of the Creator's care and concern for all the earth and its inhabitants. There is the hint in this promise that one day the waters will become a hope, a fountain leaping up to eternal life that saves instead of destroys. There is a glimpse of baptism, of the waters of resurrection and re-creation in which we have been immersed and come up gasping in the power of the Spirit. It is time to renew our commitment to life, to all of earth and its creatures, to waters that purify, heal, and save. It is time to remember that what once destroyed life now gives and sustains life.

The readings of cycle B are also about journeys from a migrant and ragtag people that became the nation of Israel, through their history and early covenants with Yahweh, to the remnant that was faithful waiting for the Messiah, to the community that came to believe in the prophet Jesus and the church. For catechumens it is the journey through the Rite of Christian Initiation of Adults (RCIA) to the celebration of the sacraments of baptism, confirmation, and eucharist at the Easter Vigil. For the larger church community it is the journey of people returning home to faithfulness and to the mission of being good news and salvation for all the world. It is the journey within and through the liturgical season of the life, passion, death, and resurrection of Jesus that culminates in the Easter Vigil, the Passover of the Lord. We begin again today and walk in the steps of many who have gone before us through the centuries, trampling down the path so that others may come after. There will be deserts, seas, promised lands, ordinary back roads, the way of the cross, the ascent to Jerusalem, the kingdom, and tombs along the way.

A prayer from the RCIA reminds us of this journeying.

God enlightens everyone who comes into the world. Through the world he has created, he makes known the unseen wonders of his love so that men and women may learn to give thanks to their Creator. You have followed his light. Now the way of the Gospel opens before you, inviting you to make a new beginning by acknowledging the living God who speaks his words of truth to all. You are called to walk by the light of Christ and to trust in his wisdom. You are called to walk in the covenant of the church, of those who believe in Jesus Christ as Lord, with those who struggle to follow him ever more closely. He asks you to submit yourself to him more and more and to believe in him with all your heart. This is the way of faith on which Christ will lovingly guide you to eternal life. Are you ready to enter on this path today under the leadership of Christ?

We walk to the cross, to the waters, to the tomb, to glory, and we walk with one another. We do not walk alone.

The responsorial psalm (Psalm 25) reminds us how to walk with this God who has accompanied us from the beginning of salvation history: "Your ways, O Lord, are love and truth, to those who keep your covenant." Our companion on the way is known for compassion, kindness, goodness, and uprightness that show sinners the way and guide the humble to justice. This is our style of walking, our way of relating to others and our attitude toward God.

In Peter's first letter we are called to be attentive and to remember Christ's death, the death of the just one, for his life and death lead us to life eternal. In Jesus Christ the life and realm of the Spirit reside, preside, and hide among us and all the earth. God is in arks, arcs, bows of hope, rainbows, life, and the hope even in prisons. With Noah there were only eight persons who made it home safely through the flood. We all know the experience of the ark through our baptisms, which are a pledge, a promise, our rainbow to God that we will live irreproachable lives through the power of the resurrection of Jesus. All heaven and earth, even the angelic rulers and powers, are now subject to Jesus Christ, who resides at the right hand of the Father. We are reminded at the beginning of our Lenten journey of this submission and order in the universe so that we can begin again with enthusiasm, power, and a renewed commitment to our baptismal promises.

This reading (like much of Paul) is multi-layered and perhaps can be more easily understood if it is couched in terms of an act of faith and a proclamation of belief. Do you believe that Christ died for our sins once and for all, so that he might bring all of us to God? Do you believe that Christ is alive in the Spirit and that he still preaches to us? Do you believe that God is patient and is waiting for you to repent? Do you believe that you are saved in baptism—not as in a ritual that removes dirt from the body, but in a ritual where God appeals to you for a clear conscience through the resurrection of Jesus? Do you believe that Jesus Christ is seated at the right hand of the Father and that all is subject to him? This is our faith, that Jesus Christ is Lord of all and that there is no place, no person, and no power that is not healed and redeemed and already under the dominion of God.

In this cycle of readings the temptation in the wilderness story is short and powerful. The Spirit sends Jesus out toward the desert. (Some translations read *drove* him out into the desert.) This is power, direction, and intent. The desert in the Jewish tradition is the place of transition between slavery and oppression and the making of a people into the children of God ready to enter into the promised land of their dreams. It is a period of testing, of letting go of what was before so that what is to come can enter into them. It is an emptying and purifying time so that the people can be formed into God's possession and become, individually and together, a people with one mind, heart, and passion. It is also a time of privilege, of intimacy with God alone, who leads and teaches them in the deepest recesses of their hearts so that they come to know that home is where God is within them.

Jesus stays in the wilderness for forty days. The number is interesting. Forty years is an adult's lifetime in most parts of the world. It is a generation for a people, as in the sojourn in the desert for the Hebrews, who were gone from Egypt but not yet ready to enter the promised land. Jesus is put to the test in this wasteland by Satan. Satan in Greek is the Hinderer; that is, anything, anyone, any event or circumstance, any decision, culture, or relationship that keeps us from fulfilling our promises and commitments, from being faithful to our covenant with the Holy One. The Latin American Sacramentary includes a list of what is to be resisted, that each person making a commitment to the community at baptism promises publicly not to be mastered by or to live in collusion with: violence, war, hatred, nationalism, racism, greed, selfishness and egoism, individualism, materialism, communism, capitalism, or any "ism," anger, dishonesty, lack of integrity, and so forth. These are the temptations that reveal if we are faithful to God and the covenant or if we have turned to the worship of idols and other forms of power.

Jesus is with the wild beasts. Angels wait on him. The wild beasts are good, not tame but good, and they serve God, not humankind intent on its own ends. The angelic powers and spirits are there, waiting to accompany us in the desert sojourn these forty days (indicative of the rest of our lives) and to serve us, as do all powers that serve God and are shared with us in our struggle against Satan, the Hinderer of the covenant.

After reflecting on who he is and how he is to bring the good news to the world, this tested Jesus will appear in Galilee proclaiming the good news of God, a covenant of hope. The powers of the world have removed the prophet John the Baptizer, the voice that came from this same wilderness and broke into the world and into our hearts. Now Jesus is ready for the time of fulfillment. The reign of God in Jesus is at hand in the presence of Jesus in the poor, among the victims of injustice, and all who suffer at the hands of the powers of the world.

The message that Jesus formulated in the wilderness, and that we will once again be called to hear and take to heart in these days of Lent is "reform your lives and believe in the good news!" *Reform* is a massive overhaul of the system, of individuals and communities, institutions and history. Remember the rainbow of harmony, peace with justice, humanity at ease with one another, with all creatures, and with God.

Our future is to be the reign of God, not a reign of greed, destruction, and violence. It is the covenant of life drawn forth from death's grip and from the destroying waters. We are to turn back to the intensity of our first love, our first belief, our first commitment. Life starts here and now. It is Lent, and God is relenting and giving us a rainbow as a sign of presence and solidarity and power. We are given angelic spirits and wild beasts for company! This journey is to be an adventure into the mystery of God's dream and hope for us and all the inhabitants of the earth.

Here are some questions for the journey: Which is more important—to get where you're going or how you travel? Do you travel with more or less than what you need? alone or with others? With whom is it good to travel? Why? Are you a good traveling companion? Where are you now? Where do you want to go in these next forty days? What do you need to give up or let go of (die to)? What do you want to take with you?

Where is the wilderness for you today? Do you look for Jesus and the Spirit in places that are hard, lonely, and difficult in your life? Do you remember that the Spirit drives us into these places, because it is here that we find out if we are really believers in Jesus, relying on God to save us and strengthen us?

The word *dominion* means "authority to rule, control; a territory controlled by a person, group; a district or area, a field of thought or activity controlled by one particular idea or person." What areas of your life does God *not* control? Why? How can you change that? *Temptation* means "to try to persuade (especially into doing something wrong or unwise) by the prospect of pleasure or advantage; to arouse a desire in, to attract, to feel inclined to do; to risk provoking by deliberate rashness." Have you given in to temptation? Do you really believe in the good news, in the covenant, or have you lost your way, not believing that God still works in your life?

What area of your life needs more good news? What area of your parish, city, and nation needs more good news? How can you bring Jesus' good news and the Spirit's power into that wilderness? Jesus only begins preaching after John the

Baptizer is arrested and cannot witness except by his presence in prison. Do we preach when politics, world events, and decisions are made against the good news?

There is a marvelous children's story called "Big Al" by Andrew Clements that can introduce us to Lent, the wilderness, and waters that save, even in the midst of trials, tribulations, and rejections.

✢ Once upon a time there was this marvelous big fish who lived in the wide blue seas. His name was Big Al. He was friendly and loved company. He was a nice fish, but poor Al was big and ugly and scary looking. He didn't look like any other fish in the sea. Every other fish in the sea had friends; some had lots, everyone had at least one. But not Big Al. He had nobody. No one would come near him or get close to him, even to talk.

But Big Al was kind and understanding, and so he didn't blame the others. But he was so lonely. He'd watch the other fish and almost without thinking swim over to a school of little fish, even medium-sized fish and immediately they would scream and scatter in a panic. He knew what he looked like: scaly, big, ugly colors, with great teeth when he smiled. He knew. He'd seen his reflection often enough—he'd just forgotten again.

But Big Al was stubborn and determined. He wanted friends. So he worked at it. He worked at great disguises. First he went the seaweed route. Round and round he wrapped it. He thought it was a great disguise, but really he only made himself bigger and greener and puffy with little eyes and big teeth. It didn't fool anyone.

Next he tried sand. He buried himself as he heard kids and even big people on land did for fun. He burrowed down (it wasn't easy with his size and his flippers) and left just his eyes and mouth above. He seemed smaller, and soon a few new fish came closer. It was great. They talked and laughed, talked about the temperature of the water and all the crazy things humans did, and Big Al was having a great time. This disguise was working! But then he sneezed (some sand got in his mouth and eyes) and after the uproar, more like a tidal wave, there wasn't another fish in sight.

Poor Al. He just didn't know what to do. But he did want friends. He tried changing colors and fading into the colors of the sea. He tried acting as if he were dead, floating and drifting. He tried never opening his mouth. (This disguise was hard, because he got awful hungry.) But nothing really worked. All this work and pretending just served to make him miserable and unhappy and that made him look even worse!

He was about ready to give up—but then something happened. What happened was pretty terrible. He'd seen it happen before, but this time he did something, without even really thinking about it. He'd been watching a whole school of little fish playing at a distance and dreaming that he'd like to be in the midst of them when suddenly a net dropped down. It was silent and deadly, and many of them were trapped.

Big Al stopped being sad and got mad. He charged right at the net and he chewed with his great teeth right through the net enabling the others to rush out through the hole. But when he headed for the hole to escape, his big body and scales got snagged. He thrashed around, but he just got more and more tangled up in the net. He was caught! All the little fish watched in dismay while their rescuer was dragged up into the light, far away from them. Big Al disappeared.

The little fish looked at each other, and when they caught their breath they talked and talked and talked about this big, marvelous, grand fish with great teeth and fiery eyes and fearless soul who had saved them all. The word spread throughout the sea. They were free, but what a shame that the great fish had been caught saving them. It was a very sad story.

But then, in the midst of the telling of the tale, there was a tremendous splash and down came Big Al, fins wagging and eyes bright and only a bit shaken up! It seems that the fishermen had taken one look at him and gasped. He was so ugly and scaly that no one would want to eat him! So they threw him back!

And now in that ocean there is a fish—a big, scary, ugly, huge, and very happy fish with more friends than anyone—Big Al.

This first Sunday of Lent is about looking at what's ugly, or apparently wild and unredeemed in us, in our lives and parishes, so that God can use that to give us friends, save other people, and bring the Spirit into the part of our life and world that needs good news and hope. The gospel talks of wild beasts. They seem to be friendly, and Jesus was with them. We have wild beasts in our lives—things we don't yet know how to tame or control, or that are different and sometimes scary. What wild beasts are alive and well in your life? And what can they do that's good?

Some of my dear friends tell me that sometimes I act like a charging rhino. I charge at things that are wrong and make a terrible noise and scare everyone half to death. So I try to think how I can be a peaceful rhinoceros, because a rhinoceros is big and strong and usually slow-moving. God wants to save everything and everyone, as in the story of Noah and the ark. Everything that was made is good, including rhinos. It's time to start making it all good again, remembering and committing ourselves to this marvelous rainbow promise of hope, of re-creation and deserts that bloom. It is Lent, the springtime of the earth and our souls.

Sunday of the Second Week of Lent

Genesis 22:1-2, 9, 10-13, 15-18
Romans 8:31-34
Mark 9:2-10

Our journey now takes us to high places, places of dreams and visions. These are places of testing and the revelations that come with letting go of those things that restrain our sight and limit our horizons. We turn to the ancient story of Abraham and the binding of Isaac. It is time to hand over to God in trust and sacrifice Abraham's most precious possession: his child. This child is his hope for the future, the tangible sign of the promise God made to him and the covenant he has with Yahweh, his lifeline to a name and a people, his security with God. Now it is time to offer the child as a holocaust, a burnt offering, so that there is nothing left in Abraham's heart and it can be given over fully to God.

The place chosen is pointed out by God. Abraham builds an altar. Then he obeys—or begins to obey. The messenger of the Lord (an angel again) stays his hand and relays a message from the Holy One: "I know now how devoted you are to God, since you did not withhold from me your own beloved son." Now Abraham gets a sense that he does not know this God who is mystery and who wants everything and will be faithful to his promises in ways that are unknown and not always easily accepted by human beings.

God knows Abraham in this binding of Isaac, and Abraham knows that he is known by God—probed, entered, seen, revealed and taken whole. It is not Isaac who is sacrificed but rather Abraham's hopes, intentions, possessions, and security. Abraham is bound more closely to God. Parts of him have been burned away by the fire of God's presence and the word that calls for unconditional and wholehearted obedience.

The Jewish community refers to this story as the binding of Isaac rather than the sacrifice of Isaac, because it marks the end of human sacrifice. God does not want to take the life of another, ever, under any circumstances. God wants us, our hearts and lives and souls.

Abraham looks around and, taking what is at hand, sacrifices to God a ram caught in the bushes. He has a need deep within to sacrifice, to worship this God. In return God extends his covenant and promise. Because of Abraham's obedience (faithfulness), God will bless him and his descendants (us) abundantly and make them as countless as the stars of the sky and the sands of the seashore.

Note all the references to the earth as connected to us, part of us, bound to us as well in this covenant, mirroring what we are like together in the eyes and heart of God.

Abraham's descendants will take possession of the gates of their enemies, and all nations of the earth will find blessing in them. And all of this will come about because of Abraham's obedience.

This is a story of hope for all of us. If this is what God promised of old, deepened and shared by not excluding God's own son and beloved child from death, then what blessings will God bestow on us this day, this Lent, this Easter? It is a time of binding, a time of promises, but a time for obedience as well, in imitation of Abraham and, of course, Jesus.

The responsorial psalm continues the journey theme with the refrain "I will walk in the presence of the Lord, in the land of the living" (Psalm 116). We walk in God's presence in the midst of affliction, death, and being bound to others. We are the servants of the Lord. We are Yahweh's faithful ones, precious in God's eyes both in life and in death. We live to offer thanksgiving and to call upon the name of our Lord. We stand in the presence of all the people and offer our promises gladly, with joy, and we dwell in the presence of God in spite of history, opposition, sin, and evil.

This sense of companionship, of safety, of being bound to God continues in Paul's letter to the Roman community. "If God is for us, who can be against us?" The emphasis is on God, not on us. Paul focuses on what God has done for us in Jesus and what God will continue to do for us and is trying to do in us even now. Life and all else come out of death! Like Abraham, we have to hear the word of the Lord and obey, even when we are afraid or do not understand. We are to believe and to trust in God's word, for it has always been reliable and true in the past, forming us and teaching us the mystery of this God who knows us and draws ever nearer to us in this season of promises and bindings. We are chosen, like Abraham, like Isaac, and like Jesus. We belong to the God of Abraham, the God of Jesus, the Father, and Jesus himself, who sits at the right hand of God and intercedes for us. This reference to the right hand means the kingdom of God is close at hand. God is close, close enough for us to lean on in our struggles and times of darkness.

The second Sunday of Lent always presents one of the accounts of the transfiguration of Jesus before Peter, James, and John. The church remembers that we are weak, so this story of resurrection glory—this glimpse of the world judged, healed, transformed, and re-created—is summoned to give us hope. Jesus takes his friends—two blood relatives and the eventual leader of his community—into a moment of glory. This is "little Easter," a moment of grace, a time of respite and strengthening, a moment of passionate delight intended to urge us through the next five weeks. If we are feeling fainthearted and nonresponsive to the season, it lifts our spirits. This is re-creation, a tying together of all the loose ends and frayed edges; it is a shining moment at the heart of creation, made glorious by the presence of Jesus at its center.

The transfiguration vision is much like the book of Daniel in which the Son of Man comes in glory; with white robes, angels, and light to judge the nations with justice; to set right the shattering of the world by sin and injustice. He is a very human person but with the power of God visible in human flesh that reveals the Spirit. Moses and Elijah, the liberator and law-giver of Israel and the prophet of expectation and future hope of the Messiah, are with him in conversation. This is the encapsulated history of an entire people standing with Jesus, the fulfillment of all that has gone before.

Peter immediately begins to talk to Jesus (oblivious in many ways to the power of the moment). "Rabbi" he calls him, teacher, unaware that Jesus is much more—lawgiver, liberator, judge, prophet, fulfillment of the Law, hope, covenant, and promises. "Rabbi, how good it is to be here. Let us erect three booths on this site, one for you, one for Moses, and one for Elijah." Peter hardly knew what to say, for they all were overcome with awe (which is true worship—silence, fear, wonder, and delight beyond words). Peter speaks for all of us. In the presence of Jesus and having lived as his disciples long after our baptisms it is still hard to understand what is going on. Then the three are overshadowed—the symbol for the power and living presence of Yahweh on earth. The word recalls the Exodus, the incarnation, and the baptism of Jesus. And the message is clear: "This is my Son, my beloved. Listen to him." When they look around, they see no one with them but Jesus.

"Listen!" This is how we are to make it through Lent to the fullness of God's vision. The way to resurrection is simple: listen. Listen to the beloved Son, the child of God, the Suffering Servant, the prophet, the judge of the nations, the testimony of God, the Word. Be still and remember Jesus is with us. Remember what God did for Abraham and his beloved child, Isaac. Remember that in Jesus we are bound tightly yet freely to this God of hope and tender regard.

We are told too that the disciples kept this word, this moment of revelation to themselves, kept it hidden. They tried to figure out what it meant, as Abraham wondered what Yahweh had in mind for him and his descendants. Lent is a time of mystery, of binding, of glory, of silence, of listening to the word of God. It is a time to remember the goodness, mercy, kindness, and power of our God, no matter who or what arrays itself against us or stands in our way, hindering us on the way of the cross to resurrection wholeness.

Our way is taken step by step, and it is taken in company with others. Jesus took his friends with him up the mountain to share his knowledge and experience of God with them. Whom do you take with you to share your understanding of God? Jesus is seen with Moses and Elijah. What law and what prophetic word do you need so that Jesus is seen to fulfill your life? This could be an individual word or one that gives heart and focus to the whole community as it walks the way together.

How do you listen to Jesus? What encourages such stillness? What areas of the good news do you not heed? Is there an area of your life that needs to be more deeply invaded by the rule of God; an area where you need to listen more closely? Who in your life can help you see God in Jesus more clearly? To whom can you talk about resurrection and what it means to live resurrection now?

The word *resurrection* means "to stand behind, to stand up for." God stood behind Jesus, behind his words, his actions, his life, and his death. God stood behind him and caught him, throwing him back into life, resisting any hold that death could have on him. Jesus' God, the Father, now stands behind us, behind our words, actions, lives, and deaths, and God also stands in between us and what we do which hinders resurrection and good news to the earth. What are you standing behind? Who are you standing behind in the world today?

Today is sometimes called the day of dreams, for God's dream for creation and for all of us is revealed in the risen Lord Jesus, beloved son raised up forever. This dream begins in baptism, and it is fraught with risks. I once had an immediate experience of what this might mean. I was swimming in the Pacific Ocean, along a wild and lonely expanse of beach off the coast of northern California. The sea was calm and full of seals playing and swimming around me. I didn't notice the current subtly shifting because I was entranced with the play of the seals. Suddenly I was caught in a rip tide. I struggled furiously for a time before I remembered that it is fruitless to fight the current. It will just wear you out and then drag you under. You have to submit and let it carry you past the ripping tide. It will take you deeper, farther out, but when the tide passes you can swim in to the shore. The seals reminded me. They didn't fight the water but eased into the pull and floated on top. I imitated them and did the same. It was a long swim into shore later, but I never would have made it otherwise. It was a terrifying feeling yet an exuberant one as well. I had been saved!

Abraham was a friend of God. God wanted all of his heart and soul, his child, his future, his trust, even when God's demands seemed to destroy Abraham's dreams and contradict God's earlier promises. Nothing was left to Abraham, and still Abraham obeyed!

God is the same with us, wanting all of us, seeing what we are and what we hold back. Our hearts are laid bare in this season. We see what we will not sacrifice and make holy for God, what we don't want to give back to God, what we want to keep for ourselves.

We are called today to listen, to obey and submit to Jesus, to offer in sacrifice all we have and what we are. In doing so, others will see through us to the glory of God. This is transfiguration—seeing through Jesus to the glory of God, and others being able to see through us, the body of Christ, to the glory of God let loose and shining in our world. Obeying transfigures our lives and radically alters our future, as it did with Abraham and Jesus. Abraham was given a nation and an unbelievable future; Jesus was given life unbounded, glory, and power.

God didn't spare Jesus from the ravages and risks of being human, and God doesn't spare us either. In baptism we have been given the privileged relationship that Jesus shared with his beloved Father, and that relationship calls us to sacrifice, obedience, trust, and risk as we walk toward God. In that closeness there is pain and suffering, even death sometimes, but the glory shines through. Jesus was full of grace and truth, yet he suffered and was condemned unjustly. We must learn in this season to see the glory of God and the presence of Jesus transfigured in those who suffer unjustly, in the friends of God who give away what is most precious to them, including their lives, and who live risking everything to save others from death, sin, and despair.

As with Abraham, God wants what is most precious to us, what we treasure more than anything else in the world. What is that? Whom do we esteem and cling to more than anyone else? What would we have to give up to belong to God alone? All these questions are asked with risk and trust believing, as the letter to the Romans states, that when we are given Jesus, all other things are granted to us as well. God intercedes for us. We are always safe; everything, every circumstance is redeemable, salvageable. Baptism and resurrection are now, not just a moment that happened once and another that will happen in death.

The transfiguration story is a way of life that we are called to imitate. We are meant to transfigure earth, our relationships, and the church, and to be transfigured by others. We are to bring life out of suffering and death; liberation and freedom out of injustice, persecution, and resistance to the gospel; light out of darkness; and hope out of despair and discouragement. This is resurrection now, shared with us in baptism and in Jesus present in the world. When we listen to Jesus and the scriptures, we learn how to obey and how to live with this seed of glory and shining grace.

When I was studying for my master's degree in systematic theology back in the early seventies I took a course on the resurrection accounts. It lasted from September through May. It was a grueling course, a heady introduction to exegesis, comparison of accounts, word plays, and so on. As Holy Week approached, we were instructed to go individually to a graveyard, tomb, or mausoleum after the Good Friday services and for at least three hours meditate and reflect on what happened to Jesus in the tomb and what resurrection means. It was a bleak, cold, windy, wet day, certainly not conducive to reflecting outdoors on anything, let alone death. I picked a huge national cemetery to get lost in and found myself in an alcove, somewhat protected from the rain and drizzle. In the midst of a half circle of stone benches there was a statue, weather-beaten and greened by age and moisture. After looking at it for ages, I still couldn't tell whether it was a man or a woman who was shrouded in mourning and abject sadness. It was haunting, a good prelude to wondering what had happened to Jesus. I sat there for hours, damp and sodden, with the cold creeping into my bones. Then I stiffly got up and headed home, knowing nothing at all.

When asked in class on Monday morning what I had learned, I said that I didn't know what happened to Jesus, that I didn't know how resurrection occurred, that I wasn't all that sure of much. I only knew that somewhere in that cold, gray afternoon with lines and lines of white crosses filling my vision I recommitted myself to believing in resurrection—as a taste, a sign, a necessary part of my life. I hoped I would grow in understanding or be given some glimpse of its meaning in the coming years. The professor accepted that, but I was left with a hunger to understand, to know so that I could stake my life on something a bit more substantial.

It was almost a decade later that I got an intimation of what it could be, this mystery of resurrection. Once again I was in class, now studying for a Ph.D. in scripture. We were examining resurrection texts and had been assigned to write a three-page paper explaining resurrection. I tried. When the wastebasket was full, I gave up and went for a walk in the nearby park. I went prepared to stay the afternoon; I brought a blanket, water, a book of poetry and my journal, dried apples, and music to take me completely away from the realms of academia. I was more attuned to a flight of fancy. I got settled in my favorite spot, one that gave me a grand view of the ocean and the fog coming in.

No sooner had Mozart started to fill the air than a busload of young boys on a field trip interrupted my fantasy afternoon. They poured out of the bus, equipped with packs, frisbees, and loud voices. I rolled over on my stomach and surveyed them as I tried to decide whether to move to another spot. But there was something about them that intrigued me. They were all between the ages of six and twelve. They were sharing food out of their sacks. Most intriguing of all, each had a huge helium-filled balloon on a long string tied to his wrist.

They played and I drifted, watching one boy in particular, about seven maybe. He was intent on everything he did. He unwrapped his brownie carefully, and he retied his shoelaces. In the midst of one such maneuver the string slipped from his wrist and the balloon headed for the skies. The boy stood there, a picture of absolute loss and dismay, as he watched his treasure slip away. His fists bunched up and his face contorted. He was just about to let out a good cry when suddenly another boy noticed the soaring balloon. He shouted: "Hey guys! look what Joshua just found out! They're better if you let them go!" In a matter of seconds forty or fifty brightly colored helium-filled balloons were all lofting away with many heads upturned, intent on watching them go. Joshua's face had gone from dismay to near ecstasy. I was stunned.

It was only a moment, but that vision has stayed with me ever since. It was the essence of resurrection. What appeared to be disastrous, without hope, utter loss and desolation for one person was redeemed by another. It was made into something unbelievably holy and delightful by those who saw the pain and let go of something precious themselves, urging all the others to share that gift. And the boy's name was Joshua! Too uncanny. I knew in a flash of a balloon soaring away and a sea of bright faces what was possible anywhere, anytime, for anyone who has eyes to see. quick reflexes, and the freedom to risk everything so another might have life. Rising helium balloons, rising hopes, and raised faces all were hints of Jesus' being raised from the dead.

I am forever grateful to that unnamed child who, in a moment of tender regard, set his friend free and taught me what rising from the dead might mean. This is our vocation. This is our command in listening to the word of the Lord. This is transfiguration. This is what binds us to earth and to the kingdom of God. We have been called to live in this sacred mystery of binding and recreating all the earth to God. It is our glory and our salvation.

Sunday of the Third Week of Lent

Exodus 20:1-17
1 Corinthians 1:22-25
John 2:13-25

The first reading begins: "God delivered all these commandments." Delivering commandments, as one would deliver a child and give birth to a new people, a nation, and a way of life; in hard labor, rendering words out of stone, hearts out of fear, and a future out of a desert band of wandering folk. This is the giving of the Decalogue, the Ten Commandments, the basis of the Jewish community's relationship with God and one another. Their actions and way of governing themselves are to be signs to other nations that they belong to Yahweh.

There is a reminder of justice and mercy, that God will inflict punishment on the children of those who hate God down to the third and fourth generations but will bestow mercy down to the thousandth generation on those who keep the commandments. The punishment is not emphasized as much as the awesome reality of the length and breadth of God's enduring mercy. Obedience to the commandments is necessary if God is to bring the people out of slavery and bondage into the way of freedom. And obedience to God's law is light to others. Freedom and living in peace with justice reveal the presence of God—with them and also with us, God's people on earth.

The list of commandments imparts a spirit and breath that is to permeate families, tribes, and the nation; it is not just for an individual's values or practice. It is the code and basis for the order and harmony that characterize belonging to the Jewish community. We, as Christians, follow Jesus' practice and observe the same Law, extending it to all people, not just to our own kind or a select few. God's mercy and saving presence in drawing the chosen people out of slavery in Egypt have been extended to all in the waters of baptism and the death of Jesus. We now fulfill the Law as Jesus did—in our lives, relationships, and communities, so that the nations will see our presence among them as a beacon of hope that lights the way to freedom. The commandments reveal the holiness of God in the life of God's people.

The responsorial psalm sums up what scripture offers us: "Lord, you have the words of everlasting life" (Psalm 19). Words can set us free, instill hope and freedom in us, in spite of what is happening in history or what is being done to us. The Law, the word of the Lord, is perfect, trustworthy, and wise; it refreshes the soul. God's commandments offer vision, truth, and justice. They are worth more than any treasure of precious metal or jewels. They are sweeter than honey. When Jewish or Muslim children practice reading aloud a portion of the Torah or the Qur'an in public, the page is smeared with honey. As the children trace the words with their finger, like a pointer, and then lick their fingers, they learn the sweetness of the word of God, making them hungry always for its taste, its incorporation and practice in their life.

Meditation on the Law leads to the discipline of harmony and careful attention to all of earth and our place in creation, not to mindless subservience. This is covenant language. We are asked to attend to the meaning of the Law, its spirit, and to seek to enflesh the words in our lives together.

The segment from 1 Corinthians is short and powerful. Like the Jews and Greeks of old, our forebears, we want signs and wisdom. But, we are reminded, we preach Christ crucified—to others an absurdity and stumbling block but to those who are called in baptism, the revelation of the very power and wisdom of God. God's folly is wiser than any of our wisdom, and God's weakness is more powerful than any strength we can muster. God's mercy and kindness to us— we who have destroyed creation, one another, and Jesus; we who have served other gods and idols and done evil and sinned, killed, hated and made enemies of other human beings—is greater than we can imagine. This reading is heartening, full of mystery and promise in our age of violence filled with destruction of human beings and the earth's resources.

Do you hear this reading, here, now? Do you demand signs and visions from God, or do you seek the wisdom of the cross and Christ crucified? Jesus Christ is the power of God and the wisdom of God, especially as the Suffering Servant, crucified and rejected. Do you believe as you look on the crucified One? Are you zealous to understand and share in the cross of Christ that sealed you in your baptism? The weakness of God is stronger than human powers and strength. Do you lean on this weakness of God that is so generous to the sinner and those who seek God? The foolishness of God is wiser than human knowledge. Do you rely on God's foolishness, which brings life out of suffering and death, and holiness out of rejection and persecution for justice's sake? Do you pray to practice this foolishness of God more completely? This is your faith. You have God's word that you are called to this power and wisdom in Jesus. Do you follow him to the cross and resurrection and encourage others on this journey?

Early in today's gospel, in the second chapter of John, lines of demarcation are drawn between the powers of darkness and light. This is a hard story, one that is not used often in the cycle of readings because of its jarring image of Jesus, who appears as the zealous, confrontational presence of God in the Temple, the Temple that belongs more to those who wield earthly power than to God. It is apparent that Jesus is on a collision course with organized religion and institutionalized worship. He stands in opposition to any group that is in collusion with the idols and powers of the world, that hinders the honor of God and the practice of justice, especially toward the least and the poorest and the weakest in the world. Passover is near—the feast that recalls the drawing of people out of slavery into freedom. And now Jesus begins to tear down the old and free people from all that enslaves them; he will destroy evil and injustice, beginning in his Father's house.

The gospel is about religion and how we mix it up with power, money, and authority. In the Temple precincts Jesus comes across people buying and selling, carrying on business that encourages the injustices of society and brings them into the holy place of God's dwelling. Jesus is forceful, angry, and decisive. He drives the money-changers out, knocking over their tables and spilling the coins. The Spirit, who drove Jesus into the desert where he did battle with Satan, the Hinderer, now drives Jesus into the Temple where he does battle with that which hinders people from worship, single-hearted devotion to God, and obedience. The passage quoted in the gospel is from Psalm 69 (cf. Jeremiah 7): "Zeal for your house consumes me!" This is holocaust language, the language of sacrifice—and it eventually will kill him. Everything must be made holy, handed over to God—beginning with the purging and purifying of religion, its practices, disciplines, rituals, and economics.

Jeremiah 7 is devastating and relentless in its accusations of the people's shallow worship and the leaders' lack of integrity, even using God to validate and endorse their greed and evil. So, we are back to signs, visions, and power, but what power? Jesus is asked by what authority, what power he does these things. His answer is convoluted and strange. Without faith in God and in God's ways of forgiveness, justice, and unconditional love, his response seems absurd. "Destroy this temple [Jesus' body] and in three days I will raise it up." His listeners are thinking pragmatically, without faith: it took forty-six years to build the Temple, and he's going to destroy it and build it up again in three days?

Jesus' answer is laced with resurrection clues and images—and his disciples and believers will remember it after Jesus' death and resurrection. They will put the pieces together then. What happens to Jesus' body happens to the body of Christ, the temple of God now—in us, individually and collectively. We must be destroyed, purified by the zeal of God, intent on making all holy. Our way of being is in the world, but not of it, so that we might be raised from the dead after three days, after the holocaust, after the surrender and sacrifice of Good Friday, when we are called to experience the death of Christ in our bodies and once again recommit ourselves to living our baptismal promises.

The signs that Jesus was performing—teaching, preaching the good news, healing, forgiving, forming community, destroying any institutional practices or social behaviors that undermine hope—fulfilled the Law given on Sinai. Superficial adherence to outward signs and devotional practices that conform to dominant cultures and majority power opinions is not the way to live out God's commandments.

The last lines of the reading from John are perhaps the most devastating as they dig deep into our souls. Jesus knows all of them—all of us—and does not entrust himself to any. He knew what was in the hearts of those who stood in his way. He knows all too well what is in our hearts, too. We are not single-hearted, or one, or holy, or consumed with zeal for our Father's house or worship or justice. This is Lent, and we are bluntly revealed for being unfaithful, sluggish of heart, divided, weak, for misunderstanding and wanting signs and wonders rather than the Word of God. We do not often truly worship God and do the justice that honors God and re-creates the world. It is time for us to acknowledge what is in our hearts and repent and rely on the power of God—the cross. We are halfway through Lent, halfway to Jerusalem, halfway to Passover and destruction, and resurrection draws nearer.

Chapters 7-8 of Jeremiah clearly express what true worship entails. Worship validates the rituals practiced in the Temple only if it is lived and honored outside of liturgy. True worship is found in living the heart of the commandments: in care for our neighbor and the poor; in respect for all people and the earth; in giving and sharing what we have been given and what has been shared with us; and in always remembering that we were brought out of slavery and are never to tolerate the enslavement of others, let alone subject them to that humiliation because of our sin and evil ways. To worship God without living truthfully and in obedience to the commandments is to dishonor God and insult and mar the image of God that we profess to worship.

Lent demands a hard look at ourselves, our parishes, and our church. We must look at our old "temples"—rules, laws, and all things that have gotten in the way of our true worship—and destroy them, die to them so that the presence of God in our lives may be true and life-giving for others. Jesus is defiant in this gospel; we too are called to defy anything and anyone that stands in the way of the true worship of God and care of all human beings. It is dangerous to be a follower of Jesus, who relies only on God's power and the power of the cross, power that is nonviolent, forgiving, merciful, power that makes peace through our own suffering and resistance to evil.

Jesus was zealous in defending God's house. For what are you zealous? Are you zealous for God's house, for the worship of God, and for God's honor and glory in public? Jesus says, in the words of Psalm 69: "Zeal for your house consumes me." What consumes you—time, work, money, worries, sports, children, marriage, gossip, insecurity, health? Jesus spoke of the Temple as his body. How do you treat the temple of your body, the temple of the Holy Spirit who dwells in you? How do you treat the bodies of others: the sick, the infirm and old, the homeless, the outcast, your enemies, those you fear and detest?

Jesus said he knew what was in the human heart. What is in your heart that Jesus does not trust, that needs to be destroyed and cast aside? Jesus was concerned with his Father's house and what was done there—worship of his Father. What kind of things do you do in worship that is not worship at all, but your own selfish agenda? When Jesus was raised from the dead, the disciples remembered his words and actions in the Temple. You have been raised from the dead in baptism. What in this gospel do you need to remember and put into practice so that Jesus is more present in your worship and church?

Today the catechumens are given the cross and signed with it again and again, for the ultimate zeal for the honor and worship of God culminates in the cross. It is good sometimes to go back to the basic ritual of such a sign, which we receive from another, in order to let it sink deep into our flesh and blood, deep down into our souls.

> Receive the cross on your forehead: by this sign of his love Christ will be your strength. Learn how to know and follow him more closely. Receive the sign of the cross on your ears: may you hear the voice of the Lord. Receive the sign of the cross on your eyes: may you see with the light of God. Receive the sign of the cross on your lips: may you respond to the Word of God. Receive the sign of the cross on your heart/breast: may Christ dwell in your heart by faith. Receive the sign of the cross on your shoulder: may you accept the sweet yoke of Christ. I sign all of you in the name of the Father, and of the Son, and of the Holy Spirit: may you live for ever and ever. Amen.

Worship that ignores the destruction of life, that seeks to avoid responsibility for standing up against evil, nonviolently, without vengeance or retaliation, is not worship. We must learn to become the sacrifice we offer and the fragrant incense that is offered to God—and we must burn. We must become holy. Doing so is never easy or quick or pleasant because of sin, evil, and our own participation in and adherence to what benefits us at the cost of others.

There is a Jewish story from eastern Europe, from the time of the Cossacks and the wanton destruction that followed in the wake of their wars and purges of the Jewish people. It is about zeal, suffering, and worship. It is not an easy story because of its brutality and truthfulness, but it is about life now in far parts of the world and in places very near home too. This is a story of the Baal Shem Tov, the master of the Good Name, who knew that he was holy and that he not only merited a seat in the kingdom of God, but that he would sit at the very hand of God, the Holy One!

✢ One day the Baal Shem Tov became curious about who would be seated on the other side of him in the kingdom of the Holy One. After all, he was going to spend forever with this person. It might be good to get to know him now, especially if he was alive in his own lifetime. So, the good rabbi approached the Holy One and asked to know who would be seated next to him. He was given a name and told that the man in question was alive and that he lived alone deep in a forest, apart from human beings, off the beaten paths of earth. From that day forward the Baal Shem Tov decided that, at first chance, he would search out this man and speak with him regarding the world and the future, especially the eternity that they would be spending together with the Holy One, blessed be his Name.

His chance soon came. He was traveling and decided to go a bit out of his way to find the man. He set off into the forest, looking for signs of a path, signs of life and habitation. It grew late. It would soon be the sabbath, and he knew that he must find refuge for the night so that he could celebrate and pray. He hoped that he soon would come upon the man's dwelling place and that he would be welcomed for the sabbath (after all, the man was a Jew—the Holy One had not indicated otherwise). Then he caught sight of the house, in the middle of nowhere, hidden away. Relieved and delighted, he approached and knocked loudly at the door.

After a long time the door opened and the Baal Shem Tov saw the largest and most unkempt man he had ever laid eyes on. The man just stared rudely, not welcoming him or speaking. Finally the Baal Shem Tov spoke, wishing the man good sabbath. The man grunted. In near desperation the Baal Shem Tov continued: "The third star is about to rise in the sky. You are a Jew; you must let me in to honor the sabbath." The man stood aside to allow him to enter but still said nothing.

The Baal Shem Tov entered and looked around. There was nothing to distinguish the hut as the house of a man who would sit next to him in the Kingdom of the Holy One. It was the Baal Shem Tov who began to recite the prayers and welcome the Sabbath Queen as he searched for a candle to light. The other man did nothing but sit alone.

When the prayers were finished and it grew darker in the dimly lit cabin the man pulled himself to his feet and began to root around, taking food out of every nook and corner, from under the beds, out of the cabinets, closets, everywhere. He piled it on tables, chairs, beds, and then he proceeded to eat and eat and eat. The Baal Shem Tov stood and watched, stunned. He was offered nothing; the man kept eating, seemingly oblivious to his presence. Finally, he meekly asked for something, and the other threw him a crust of bread. Afterward, the man stacked everything in a corner and went to bed. So the Baal Shem Tov found himself a place to sleep in a corner and cleared it as best he could.

The man puzzled him and disturbed him greatly. The Almighty, blest be his Name, had told him in confidence that this man was holy and would dwell with him in the Kingdom, close to him forever. He watched the man, remembering that there are those who hide their holiness from the prying eyes of the world. Perhaps the man would get up in the middle of the night and pray for the world, wailing or sitting in silent vigil. He was still reeling from the fact that the man didn't celebrate the sabbath—not even with rudimentary prayers or acknowledgment of the holy time of rest. The Baal Shem Tov stayed awake most of the night, watching and waiting, but the other man slept soundly, snoring loudly, and was still sleeping at the coming of the light when the Baal Shem Tov rose to pray.

All day the Baal Shem Tov kept the sabbath, and the other man grunted and wandered about the cabin, periodically taking out more food from hidden caches in the cabin, eating and eating and eating, only throwing a bit to the Baal Shem Tov when he coughed or indicated that he was hungry too. Nothing was spoken between them. Again, night fell and the Baal Shem Tov watched to see if the man's behavior would change at all. But there was nothing to indicate that he was holy or that the Almighty was honored by his presence in the world.

The next morning the Baal Shem Tov prepared to continue his journey, baffled and very upset in soul. He decided he must say something to this man with whom he has spent the last hours. He awkwardly approached the door, hand on the latch, turned to him, and blurted out: "Do you know who I am?" The man grunted affirmatively. "And I know who you are!" the Baal Shem Tov added. "I have spoken with the Lord of heaven and he has told me about you—that you are holy unto the Lord and that he hears you. But I don't understand. You don't appear holy. You do not observe the sabbath. You do not pray. You do not keep vigil. You do not even practice hospitality! Who are you? Why do you live like this?"

The man didn't reply for the longest time, his head hung close to his chest. Then he raised his eyes and looked straight into the Baal Shem Tov's eyes and spoke: "It was a long time ago, and I was but a boy, maybe seven or eight. I lived here with my mother and father, two sisters, my grandfather and grandmother. We were happy. We were poor, but we lived well. There was water and food, and we had one another.

"Then one day I was out with my father. We had gone deeper into the forest to the spring to fetch water. Suddenly my father pushed me and then shoved me under a fallen tree, hissing that I must keep still and not come out—no matter what. I hid, and many horsemen came. They dragged my father away. I heard the screams of my mother and sisters and grandmother as they were attacked. I crawled out of the tree and crept through the forest. They had my father. They tied him to a tree, and they tortured him horribly. They taunted him and tried to get him to deny the Holy One, to profane his Holy Name. Eventually they poured fuel over him and set him on fire. My father was a small, thin man, and he burned fast. The flames went out quickly, and it was over. The Cossacks left, and I was left alone.

"I came back and buried what was left of the bloodied bodies of my family. I stayed. I live here now. But I made myself a promise. When the Cossacks come again—and they will come again, for they always do—they will find me and take me and tie me to a tree. But I won't go so quickly. I will be so huge, so fat, so strong that when they put the match to me, I will burn and burn, hot and furious. I will burn long, crying out and praising the name of the Holy One. They will hear my words screaming in their ears, and I will refuse to burn out. I will just keep burning."

There was a long silence. The great hunk of a man stood before the Baal Shem Tov with great tears running down his face, and then he began to pray, oblivious once again to the Baal Shem Tov.

"O God, Lord and Master of the Universe, how long? How long will your people continue to kill and slaughter one another? How long, O Lord, will you suffer us and stand by and watch us destroying your creatures made so lovingly? How long, O Lord, will you weep over your children and their fights and hatreds. How long, O Lord, how long?"

The Baal Shem Tov withdrew as quietly as he could, pulling the door shut behind him. He walked a few steps back toward the road and his old life, and then he stopped dead in his tracks. For the first time in his life the great and holy Baal Shem Tov, master of the Good Name, wondered if *he* was worthy to sit next to this man in the Kingdom of heaven for all eternity. He left with the man's cry of anguish and prayer ringing in his ears and wringing his heart.

This story is about zeal for our Father's house, for the body of Christ, for human beings made in the image and likeness of God, men and women that God cherishes and expects us to do the same. Worship is about caring for one another, and ritual must serve to remind us of true adoration of God: thanksgiving for life, gratitude expressed in sharing its riches, and communion with one another. This is the fulfillment of the Law, the commandments, the Spirit at the heart of Jesus' way of worshiping his Father. We are invited this Sunday of Lent to pray for the virtue and practice of zeal so that our worship will be acceptable to God, the Father Almighty.

Sunday of the Fourth Week of Lent

2 Chronicles 36:14-17, 19-23
Ephesians 2:4-10
John 3:14-21

We keep repeating the same old story of sin in our own lives and history; governments, priests, and people alike add infidelity to infidelity, ignoring the Ten Commandments and continuing to pollute the earth, peoples' hearts and lives. as well as the Temple. That is the real horror, the sin—that we have been consecrated to God by baptism, confirmation, and eucharist, and yet we turn away.

This reading is about the community and its absolute need for repentance and judgment. We are a people, and we betray God together. publicly. All the nations see our hypocrisy, because basically we act like them, not like the people of God. We claim to belong solely to God, and yet we are intent on "making it" in the world as others do—through violence, nationalism, materialism, greed, hatred, and all the rest of the litany of sin that is shared by peoples the world over.

God has sent messengers often, insistently, imaginatively, for God has compassion on the earth and on us. But we have scoffed at the prophets, persecuted them, and killed them to avoid listening to the truth. We don't want to hear of God's dismay at what we are doing to creation and to one another, usually at the same time we are professing that we are good God-fearing people. Even war, destruction, famine—like the loss of the Temple for the Jews—don't seem to get through to us. We don't see that these evils result from our decisions and actions, from ignoring God's commandments.

Somehow it seems that God pulls back, seemingly ignoring us. When that happens, anyone and everyone can get at us. But God is attentive, mindful, even—or especially—in

these times, waiting for any intimation that we might turn
again and reach out in our pain and need for God's grasp.
God waits on us, and still we delay, following selfish and evil
ways.

The prophet Jeremiah warned:

> "Until the land has retrieved its lost sabbaths, during all
> the time it lies waste it shall have rest while seventy
> years are fulfilled."

The people of his time did not keep holy the sabbath or honor
the Law that held them together as a people in the promised
land and reminded them of their sojourn in the desert and
their time of bondage in Egypt. They had forgotten and acted
like those who once oppressed them and held them in con-
tempt.

So the decree of God in the mouth of the prophet is announced—there will be seventy years of rest, rest from the
abomination of living like the rest of the nations while still
claiming to worship God in the Temple. And it indeed comes
to pass that Cyrus, king of Persia, commissions the rebuild-
ing of the Temple in Jerusalem to the honor of God. His proclamation reads: "Whoever, therefore, among you belongs to
any part of his people, let him go up, and may his God be
with him!" An outsider acknowledges God and frees anyone
who belongs to him to go and be with God, belong once
again to God's people. God works wonders and mighty deeds,
even in foreigners. What then can God do with us, God's
own people, if we are attentive?

So images of what is to come, hints of the future, are found
in history and in the stories of the people: images of being
beloved children of God, of God among us, and of God liber-
ating us so we can belong once again to a people that serves
God alone and worships rightly, justly, and wholeheartedly.
This is the word of the Lord. You'd think we'd get the message!

Bosnia, Palestine, Northern Ireland, Oklahoma City, New
York City reverberate with the sound of bombs, screaming
children, and innocent people. The land itself struggles to
survive along with the creatures of water, air, and forest. This

is our story, the chronicle of the twentieth century. We have slaughtered more human beings in a hundred years than in the entire previous history of the human race, all too often in the name of a deity, in the name of the God who gives life and seeks only to give us new hearts of flesh instead of stone. We do homage to idols and machines of war while stubbornly claiming that we believe in God. Ours is an appalling story.

The responsorial psalm reminds us of what we should do: "Let my tongue be silenced, if I ever forget you!" (Psalm 137). We *do* forget, often and for long periods of time. The psalm is a dirge, a lament of exile and loss:

Once we sat and wept and we remembered and we hung up our harps on the aspen trees and refused to sing the songs of our land and beloved city of peace and hope. . . . How can we sing? If we forget then we might as well forget that we have hands and tongues and a life. Jerusalem, the dwelling place of God, the city of peace with enduring justice, is more important than any individual's joy or personal happiness (my paraphrase).

The lament even begs God to make our tongues stick to the roofs of our mouth, silencing us if we forget the goodness of God. But we have forgotten!

The letter of Paul to the Ephesians begins with the refrain that brings back the joy and redeems all of us:

God is rich in mercy; because of his great love for us he brought us life with Christ when we were dead in sin.

God is rich in mercy is a mantra that we must learn to chant, to sing in harmony, to breathe in and out, to remember in our very bones.

The readings remind us that we were dead—dead in sin, dead in injustice, dead with insensitivity, dead to worship, dead in wars and famine, dead in hate—and now we have been brought to life again in Christ Jesus, who is the ultimate kindness of our God. We have been saved by a favor, a grace, a mercy beyond telling or understanding. We are raised up now, and we have a place in the kingdom of heaven. God's favor is shown in kindness to us, and through us to the world. This is not our doing, but God's gift, God's work. We are being refashioned, re-created in Jesus Christ to lead a life of good which God has prepared for us from all time. It is time for us to get on with it—Lent is sliding away from our grasp. Now is the time to remember, to take heart and to chant our mantra: God is rich in mercy. . . . God is rich in mercy. . . .

The gospel relates the mysterious story of the teacher Nicodemus, who comes secretly to Jesus to discuss his teachings and to probe the Master on his belief in God. He comes at night, in the darkness, to sit in the presence of the light of the world. Jesus' preaching to Nicodemus reminds us of our own traditions and beliefs, blurred and often forgotten, laid aside in the presence of a secular culture, occupying forces, other nations' idols, and our own weakness and failure to honor our commitments both publicly and privately.

Jesus' words here are powerful: "Yes, God so loved the world that he gave his only Son, that whoever believes in him may not die but may have eternal life." They are deeper still when taken in the context of the discussion. The image is that of Moses, the liberator and the giver of the Law, lifting up a serpent wrapped around a pole so that the people who have sinned by cursing Moses and God can look on what is killing them, biting them as they have bitten one another with stinging words that undermine hope and belittle God's ways. They complained about the manna in the desert, which sustained them, which was in fact the presence of God caring for them, and they disdained God's gift of life, of freedom, of a promise, of a future.

They must learn to look at their sin and see the results of their behavior and the destructive nature of their words upon one another. In looking, in truly seeing, they will be saved. By acknowledging their sin they will be set free and given health and life; they will be able to go on. This image calls to our mind the Son of Man, who will be lifted up on the cross so that all of us may look upon what we have done to God's beloved Suffering Servant and son, what we have done to one another for all of history, what we continue to do today. To see the crucified One, the one belonging solely and utterly to God, suffering because of our collusion with evil and our sin is the beginning of salvation. Jesus' way is the way home, the way out of horror and inhumanity and infidelity, the way to one another in grace and freedom. If we do not look upon Jesus and confess our sins then we choose to remain in the hateful and destructive way of death that permeates all of history.

The image is extended into the contrast between light and dark. Light entered the world but we preferred the darkness: injustice, violence, greed, selfishness, viciousness, insensitivity, hypocrisy, and all manner of evil deeds. The lines are drawn; those who practice evil hate the light and do not come near it for fear their deeds will be exposed, but those who act in truth come into the light to make clear that their deeds are done in God. There are two choices only: darkness and hate and evil deeds, or light and deeds done in God and truth to be told and proclaimed. It is late in Lent and time for us to choose. Not to choose is to choose evil.

It is time to look on the crucified One as our ancestors looked on the serpent in the desert. In looking and seeing, we, like our ancestors in the desert, will be healed, forgiven, and saved. Our story continues the stories of Noah, Abraham, Exodus, Moses, Elijah, Cyrus, Jeremiah, the destruction of the Temple, and so forth—all crucial stories where God has been working mysteriously, hidden in all of history and all events to save us again and again.

We are exhorted to believe, to keep going in trust, to endure gracefully, to remember. Jesus will be hung on a cross, but all who look on him in his suffering and death and who confess their collusion with sin and its terrible effects on the innocent will be saved. God has sent the Son into the world to save us. Belief in Jesus is the beginning of our practice of unconditional love, belief in nonviolent resistance to evil, belief in the cross. With Jesus we lay down our lives for the truth, the honor of God, and one another. Love will save us and the earth again.

Condemnation—not to believe in God's way of living—is failing to put into practice this story of love, this law of for-

giveness and mercy that has been extended to us. It is refusing to grasp hold of God, choosing to live instead by extin-
guishing the light within us and the world, taking the lives of
others, serving evil, practicing injustice. It is being mastered
by sin rather than steadfastly standing in the light, signing
oneself and others with the sign of the cross.

Today is a time of light, a harsh light, the light that glares
on the cross. We will all be exposed for our part in evil and
our refusal to stand against the darkness. Our deeds and our
hearts will be exposed. Do we live by God's favor and Jesus'
obedience to God in being human with us, subject to death
and the effects of our choices in the world—or do we live by
evil, courting the darkness? It is time to be revealed, laid
bare. Where do we stand, under the shadow and the sign of
the cross or over and against it, aligned with other powers
and other gods?

Nicodemus traditionally came under cover of darkness
because he didn't want to be known publicly as a follower of
Jesus. He was still uncommitted. Sometimes we act the same
way—hiding in the shadows, hiding our doubts and weak
faith from others. But we are called to live in the light and let
others see our deeds so that God's glory is revealed in our
lives. We are called to be courageous about our faith, to be
more public about our commitment to the light, the truth,
justice and peace, to the common good of others.

Later in John's gospel Nicodemus attempts to stand up
for Jesus, reminding the Sanhedrin that a man must have a
trial before he is judged. But he quickly disappears again in
the shadows when they ask whether he is a follower of Jesus
or of the Law of Moses. It is only after the resurrection that
he became a follower of Jesus. This Sunday asks us where
we stand publicly on issues of belief, suffering and death,
especially suffering that is incurred because of our association with the struggle for the Kingdom, the gospel, and on
behalf of others.

There is a story told in many countries about letting others know where we stand. It is a story popular with groups
seeking to make changes and to get us to think about our
beliefs and our position in society.

✢ Once upon a time there was a small group of people who sought to bring change to their country. They analyzed the current situation and its effects on certain segments of society. They concluded that the government, schools, and churches were not being honest and that those most in need were not being taken care of and included in decisions. So they spoke out, held public meetings, organized, and met in small groups to discuss what should happen.

One Sunday morning they decided to picket in front of the churches, while one person handed out leaflets stating their positions. But word had leaked out that they were going to do this, and police were waiting at every place they showed up. There were scuffles, confrontations, beatings, hard feelings, shouting matches, and many arrests. Unfortunately, brutal and unnecessarily violent measures were used. Still, church and government leaders thought they had handled the situation rather efficiently without letting the good church-going people be bothered by such "riffraff." They had moved quickly, with force. They had provided a lesson for anyone who might think to do such things in the future.

The years went by, and the situation in the community worsened. The poor got poorer while the rich got richer. There was an increase in the sales of home security systems and the purchase and carrying of weapons for protection. There was a higher incidence of crime and brutalization of certain groups. Racism was rampant. Many citizens blamed those newly arrived in the country or different from the dominant culture and ruling groups for the problems. There was general uneasiness, as though life was really a time-bomb with a long fuse that was fast coming to the end—ready to explode everywhere.

There was a man—a teacher, prophet, and leader—who was saddened by the state of affairs. He had written and prayed publicly, called people to repent, told stories of conversion, and sided with the outcasts. He would talk to anyone who approached him. He was insightful, demanding on occasion, and always truthful whether it was convenient or not. He remembered what had happened long ago to those who had sought to pass out leaflets and picket the churches.

He started showing up at cathedrals, synagogues, public receptions, and government affairs, handing out papers silently to anyone and everyone. The officials quickly shuffled him away, handcuffed and arrested, but as soon as he was out of jail, he would go to another place and do it again. They couldn't really accuse him of anything because the papers were always blank. There was absolutely nothing on them.

The number of his followers grew. When asked what he was doing, he said simply: "I give out empty papers like all the empty words, promises, and actions of people. I go to places others have gone before, so that people will remember what happened then. Perhaps some will decide where they stand and remember what it is that they profess. For some the light will go on; others will have to choose consciously to turn the light off."

Today is traditionally called Laetare Sunday, the day of rejoicing, the point in Lent where we turn more deliberately into the light. The forces arrayed against Jesus become clearer, and Jesus' way of light and truth is delineated in opposition to all those who live with infidelity and worship idols. It is a Sunday of warning and a call to look with eyes wide open at the reality of our evil and how it culminates in the cross of Christ. It is a call to look around at the world today and see how that horror still continues in the crucifixion of so many others because of our sin.

Perhaps one way to look, truly see, and confess is to pray together in the dark, eyes closed. Gather in a small room or darkened church or chapel. The brief litany that follows is a service against darkness, naming abominations and praying for all the world so that the light can grow stronger.

Reader. We continue on our journey to the light, to the Easter Vigil, looking at our world and at our own lives in the light of Christ, who is lifted up before us on the cross.

Leader: Let us pray. Lord, be close to your family. Rule and guide us on our way to your Kingdom and bring us all into the light of your truth.

Response: Let us see you, Lord!

Leader: Let us kneel.

We will be saved, but on our knees and under the sign of the cross. (*Let us see you, Lord.*)

Let us pray for all those who do evil and all those who do not challenge evil. (*Let us see you, Lord.*)

Let us pray for all those who are complacent and passive. (*Let us see you, Lord.*)

Let us pray for all those who are concerned only with their own lives. (*Let us see you, Lord.*)

Let us pray for all those who in their greed steal life from the poor. (*Let us see you, Lord.*)

Let us pray for all those who blame the homeless and aliens for their predicament. (*Let us see you, Lord.*)

Let us pray for all those who use war and hatred in their attempt to control. (*Let us see you, Lord.*)

Let us pray for all those who use violence and vengeance to get their way. (*Let us see you, Lord.*)

Let us pray for all those who legally kill and thus add to fear and insecurity in the world. (*Let us see you, Lord.*)

Let us pray for all those who are not moved by the starvation and sickness of children and the poor. (*Let us see you, Lord.*)

Let us pray for all those who practice and encourage abortion, euthanasia, and the death penalty. (*Let us see you, Lord.*)

Let us pray for all those who self-righteously blame others and take no responsibility for the evil in the world today. (*Let us see you, Lord.*)

Let us pray for all those who use and sell drugs and alcohol, and who seek profit from prostitution. (*Let us see you, Lord.*)

Let us pray for all those who nurture hatred and refuse to forgive. (*Let us see you, Lord.*)

Let us pray for all those who are sources of division in the world and in the church. (*Let us see you, Lord.*)

Let us pray for all those who use their authority for their own ends instead of serving others. (*Let us see you, Lord.*)

(*Add other petitions, if desired. Then remain in silence on knees for several moments.*)

Leader: Let us pray.

That you, O Lord, may dispel the darkness of our minds and be the light that shines in the hearts of your people. Let us pray to the Lord. (*Lord, hear our prayer.*)

That you may kindly lead us to Christ, the Light of the world, let us pray to the Lord. (*Lord, hear our prayer.*)

That we may open our hearts to God and acknowledge you as the source of light and the witness to the truth, let us pray to the Lord. (*Lord, hear our prayer.*)

That you may heal us and preserve us from the skepticism of this world, let us pray to the Lord. (*Lord, hear our prayer.*)

That you, who take away the sin of the world, may free us from the contagious power of evil, we pray to the Lord. (*Lord, hear our prayer.*)

That after having been enlightened by the Holy Spirit, we may never fail to profess the good news of salvation and share it with others, we pray to the Lord. (*Lord, hear our prayer.*)

That all of us, by the example of our lives, may ourselves become in Christ the light of the world, we pray to the Lord. (*Lord, hear our prayer.*)

That all the inhabitants of the earth may acknowledge you as the creator of all things, the One who bestows upon us the gifts of the Spirit and life ever more abundantly, let us pray to the Lord. (*Lord, hear our prayer.*)

Let us pray. Lord God, unfailing light and Father of light, by the death and resurrection of your Son, Jesus, you have cast out the darkness of hatred and deceit and poured upon the human family the light of truth and love. Hear our prayers for the sons and daughters you have called and chosen to be your very own children. Help us pass from darkness to radiance. Set us free from the power of the prince of darkness, so that we may live forever as children of the light. We ask this through Christ, our Lord. Amen.[1]

Blessing:

You are the light of the world. Go in peace and shatter the darkness with your light. In the name of the Father and of the Son and of the Holy Spirit. Amen.

---

[1] See *Rite of Christian Initiation of Adults*, pp. 165-66.

Sunday of the Fifth Week of Lent

Jeremiah 31:31-34
Hebrews 5:7-9
John 12:20-33

The reading begins with hope, with a look to the future that hints that whatever is coming is close at hand. What is coming is a new covenant with Israel and Judah and with the Holy One. It is not like any of the covenants of old. The people have been taken out of slavery and into freedom, but that covenant was broken. Now there will be another covenant built on the old foundations, and this covenant will be extended within the house of Israel and to all its descendants and believers, after those days of unfaithfulness. This covenant will be written in flesh and blood. The Law will be internalized, integrated into all aspects of relationships, life, worship, commerce, and so on: "I will be their God, and they shall be my people."

It will come to pass. It is a declaration and a promise. All, from the least to the greatest in the land, shall know God, and God will forgive their evil ways and remember their sin no more. There will be more passionate promises and unbounded forgiveness, and once again God intends to make the people holy and claim them again as God's alone. All of us and all the earth will be intimate with God. The mystery comes closer and closer. The Kingdom, the original intent of creation and of life, is moving toward fulfillment in Jesus, in history, in the Spirit, in us.

Our response to this covenant is to acknowledge how far we have to go as a people. We pray in Psalm 51 (a penitential lament): "Create a clean heart in me, O God." We stand before God, clinging to God's goodness and great compassion, aware of our need for mercy. We need our smudged faces and dirty hands washed and our hearts purified. In this process of being made clean we learn what steadfastness is:

courage and endurance. In attending to God's presence in our lives, joy returns to us. We pray for a willing spirit, so that others who sin and transgress as we have done will return to God. It is our place to teach others the ways of God. They can take heart from us as we take heart from Jesus' faithfulness and obedience to God.

The Letter to the Hebrews reminds us that Jesus offered prayers and supplications to God with loud cries and tears, and God heard him because of his reverence. Verse 7 powerfully reveals what our own inner attitude toward God should be: one of reverencing God. We are to imitate Jesus' words, "I revere my Father" (John 8:49). This is the essence of Jesus' strength, prayer, and way of being in the world.

In the midst of this season of Lent, the springtime of our souls, we pray to learn that same position of adoration, of worship. More soberly, we are reminded that "Son though he was, he learned obedience from what he suffered; when perfected, he became the source of eternal salvation for all who obey him" (Hebrews 5:8-9). This is succinct and all-encompassing. This is to be our attitude for the rest of Lent: crying out to God with tears, prayers, and supplication in reverence and obedience to God. We too must learn to obey, to listen, to put into practice wholeheartedly, to offer ourselves as a sacrifice to God in worship.

We return to John once again. It is Passover and many come to worship in the Temple, including some Greeks. They approach Philip and put a request to him: "Sir, we would like to see Jesus." (Remember that truly seeing Jesus is salvation itself.) Philip goes to Andrew and Andrew goes to Jesus and Jesus goes to them. It is like a child's game of connect the dots; these lifelines hook people together, pulling them into the circle of discipleship. It is a pattern, a way of life for those of us who call ourselves Christians, part of the company of Jesus. We need each other to see Jesus, to be saved. Jesus comes to us through others, through the lifelines, through other members of the community. And Jesus tells these Greeks, these outsiders: "The hour has come for the Son of Man to be glorified." This is the hour of revelation, the hour of the cross, the hour of testing. In the midst of the darkness the light will break.

The image Jesus uses to describe his own destiny (and so ours as well) is the grain of wheat that must fall to the earth and die. Otherwise it remains just a grain of wheat. But if it dies, if it is buried in the soil, watered by time, weather, and spirit, nurtured by the hard work of God and humankind, it produces much fruit. Jesus is talking about his own death on the cross and burial in a borrowed tomb. Contrary to appearances, his death is life for all, because God will hear his cry and accept his love.

This reading is also about our baptisms, when we died to all else but the power and life of God and live only to bring that life to others. Jesus is talking about the process of denying our very selves and picking up our crosses and bearing our share of the burden of the good news in our flesh so that others might have life. Jesus is clear that those who love their life and cling to it will lose it, while those who let go of life in this world will preserve their life forever. If we would serve Jesus and preserve our lives then we must follow him to the cross, to foot washing (service), and there, where the servant is, Jesus is found.

The body of Christ is found at the cross, at the washing of the feet, in the corporal works of mercy, in the making holy of the world and its structures. The Father will honor anyone who follows Jesus. Think of that: The Father will serve and honor us as Jesus honors and reveres the Father! The relationship shifts and is reversed so that once again, unbelievably, our God bends before us and seeks to be intimate with us. To serve others is to serve Jesus, to imitate Jesus' God who served us best in Jesus' life and suffering and death.

There is a story from China, based on accounts given in the early part of this century, when once again the Far East opened its doors a crack to the West. It is about the first Christians in China, in the late sixteenth century.

✢ A missionary priest came through a remote mountain pass to a village that was isolated and unaware of anything that happened outside its terraced valley. The word of the Lord was preached, and a small handful of the villages became believers and banded together, encouraging one another and praying the scriptures daily. They celebrated the Eucharist for as long as they could and when the priest died, they fed each other on the words and stories that they had learned by heart.

Life was hard. They were poor, like the others in the village, and they were looked upon with suspicion and avoided. This pained them, for the other villagers were their families, relatives, and friends. They wanted to be accepted, to live in peace and harmony together, but even more they wanted their kin and neighbors to know the power of God, the sense of joy and freedom that the gospel had given to them.

For many nights they met to tell the stories and to pray, and then they begged the Spirit for an answer. What could they do to help their neighbors see them more clearly, not as enemies and traitors and to be feared and excluded, but as friends and, hopefully, friends of God? Already they had been pushed to the far edges of the village and made to work only the terraces highest up on the mountain, far away from the well. As they struggled with their pails and baskets strung on poles they were ridiculed and stared at. Sometimes, depending on events in the village, stones, pebbles, dung, or garbage were thrown at them. It was becoming unbearable.

At last an old woman spoke. "I know exactly what we have to do, but you won't like it! I certainly didn't when the Spirit suggested it to me. I know it isn't my idea. I would never have thought to do something like this." They pressed her for her suggestion, saying that they would be open to her words and reflect on her suggestion in the light of the gospel. Her revelation, born of the Spirit, was this: They would all get up earlier and instead of climbing the steep terraced sides of the mountain to water their own patches of land, they would begin with those closest to the well, watering their neighbors' patches of land. They would work their way out from the well and only do their own small pieces of ground last. The people were speechless. It was a horrible idea: exhausting, demeaning, stupid. Their neighbors would think they had gone mad. Why would they water the plots of those who insulted them and demeaned them, or, at best, ignored them?

But they prayed and when the vote was taken, not a soul objected. So, they prayed for strength and resolved to begin early the next morning, after Sunday's rest.

Before dawn they gathered, blessed each other, and began carrying water to the fields immediately next to the well—the fields that were the largest and the best cultivated, those belonging to the richest members of the community. Trip after trip they moved back and forth, slowly working their way up the mountain sides. When the sun rose and their neighbors came out, they laughed themselves silly, bending over with tears running down their faces, pointing at them. They took the day off. These crazy Christians—no one ever knew what they would do next.

The next morning was the same, and every day after that. The Christians barely had time to water their own fields, working as the sun went down. They barely prayed, except for the Our Father, and then they slept and rose the next morning to start again. On Sunday the Christians rested, near collapse.

The second week the villagers lined up to watch them, this time mostly in silence, wondering, asking why. There were very few harsh words, and toward the very end of the week a child about ten years of age joined them as they carried water painfully up to their own fields.

The third week a few more people joined them instead of letting them do all the work, though very few continued working into the night with them. As the weeks wore on, more and more of the villagers worked with them and stayed to carry water to the very top of the mountain.

It took six months before the villagers realized that the Christians were going to keep at this: serving them gladly, helping them, and putting their neighbors' needs before their own. And then the villagers began to come to pray, to listen to the stories on Sunday, and finally to be baptized, to follow Jesus, the Suffering Servant of God.

Within a few years the whole village hidden in the mountains was baptized, was made Christian. When missionaries finally came upon the small valley in the middle of the twentieth century, nearly four centuries later, they were still Christians. They described themselves as water-carriers and told the story of how they had become believers. They told those who came that Christians were those people who watered their neighbors' fields first and then invited them to the water and the bread of joy and community service.

These Chinese Christians were like the first Christians who learned in their flesh that "unless the seed falls into the ground and dies it remains just a seed, but if it is buried then it bears much fruit." They translated the story of the seed into service to others and so to the Father of us all.

This reading is multilayered. After explaining what will happen to him and what is meant to happen to all of us, ritually and in reality, Jesus begins to pray aloud: "Father, save me from this hour?" Note the question mark. It was for this hour that Jesus was born. All time and history have led to this moment. He prays with intensity: "Father, glorify your name!" In Jesus' life and death—and in our lives and deaths, handed over to God in service, witness, and alliance with the victims of injustice and solidarity for the poor—is the glorification, the worship, and the true honoring of God. It is the worship and sacrifice that God wants from us, no matter what it may cost us, even our lives.

The voice from the sky, as in Jesus' baptism, reassures Jesus that God is with him, that God will indeed glorify his name again in his life and offering and death. The crowd hears the voice as thunder. Jesus says that the voice comes not for his sake but for ours, heartening us again to face what lies before us all in Jerusalem on Palm Sunday and Holy Week, which is close upon us. The hour is near!

What is to come is the cross and the hour of glory. We are to worship God in the life and death of Jesus, who is faithful to the covenant written in the hearts of human beings. His obedience is not only to God, but to the limits of being human and being in relationship with others who are slow to understand the presence of God among us. It is time to fulfill our baptismal promises and God's covenant to us in Jesus' death and resurrection.

Now judgment comes upon the world. The prince of this world, the Hinderer, will be driven out by the power of the Spirit that drove Jesus into the desert, into the Temple, up the mountain. This same Spirit now drives him to set his face toward Jerusalem and the cross. Jesus speaks again: "And I—once I am lifted up from the earth—will draw all to myself." The cross is the place where the balance is restored, the center is fixed, and the earth comes together. It is the place of death, the death of Jesus and the ultimate death of evil and sin and selfishness for the powers of the world. It is the place of life, of hope, of the seed blossoming forth, of abundant life, of the covenant fulfilled mysteriously in the wisdom of God.

We too are confronted with the hours of our lives. What was the worst or the hardest hour? What was the best hour? It is in these extreme hours that we see most clearly what our deepest sin is—and what the Spirit of God can do in us.

Jesus prays aloud, "My soul is troubled." When Jesus is troubled, he turns to his Father and prays. He doesn't demand that God save him from trouble, from hard times, from pain and suffering, or even from death. Instead, he asks that all he does will glorify God and focus others' eyes on God. He prays to show others the goodness and mercy, the steadfastness of God, especially in hard times, the times of violence, unnecessary death, betrayal, and hatred.

This is what our religion is all about. We believe that because of the cross every moment, every hour, every situation, every person is redeemable and can bring glory to God. Our lives, our sufferings, our fears, even our deaths can be a source of life, hope, and strength for others and bring others to belief, for that is what Jesus has done for us. Jesus' hour is the source of all our belief and strength.

We should be troubled about the same things that Jesus is troubled about: injustice, deceit, hard-heartedness, greed, violence, the lack of medical care, food, housing, shelter, clean water and hope for people. We should be troubled about nationalism, racism, and regional conflicts that scream out from our televisions and papers, about the assassinations and rampant killing of one group of people by another. We should be troubled about gang initiations, drive-by shootings, concealed weapons, inflammatory commercials, and political campaigns, about blaming others for our own greed and rudeness and coarseness of speech and entertainment. This fifth week of Lent is a good time to look deeply into our hearts and into our families and loved ones, our friends and parishes, our communities and cities, our nation.

This is also a time to reflect upon how we learn obedience. Perhaps when we were small we played a game called Simon Says. The game requires listening to the words carefully in order to do what is commanded. But always there was a time the order was given without the phrase "Simon says"—and we did it anyway. Unfortunately, we continue to live a lot like that as we grow older. We do what others say, often without even thinking about whether it is connected to our faith, to the scriptures, to the commands of God. We do it because of others' values rather than the values of Christ.

We are journeying in the company of Jesus, and there are others trying to get to Jesus through us, just as the Greeks came to Philip and then through Andrew and on to Jesus. We are a lifeline. Whom are we holding onto? Whom are we passing on to Jesus? Whom are we really obeying? Who needs our service now—an AIDS hospice, soup kitchen, rest home, a single parent at your child's school, a mother with young children who would rejoice in a day off, a teen seeking support and a sense of identity and power, older people who would love to go to church next week but are afraid to go out or can't drive?

Being a servant is a full-time job, a vocation that is to be threaded through all else that we plan on doing. The covenant asks if we are the people of God, with God's Law written on our hearts. Can anyone tell? Are we the servants of the Lord, willing to help others bear their burdens and to walk with them on their way to Jerusalem? This is the way of the cross. Simon of Cyrene was enlisted, dragged into helping Jesus carry his cross; under duress he learned obedience and was saved.

This is a good time to go to the sacrament of reconciliation. This is the hour for us to come together in communion with others to pray and prepare for Holy Week, and to
live so as to invite others to the presence of Jesus. We
need to share with those we love and those with whom we
worship how we have learned obedience in our suffering,
how we have learned to lay down our lives for another. The
reading from Hebrews, rewritten as a proclamation of faith,
instructs us on the way.

> Do you remember and believe that while Jesus was in
> the flesh he offered prayers and supplication with loud
> cries and tears to God?
>
> Do you, in imitation of Jesus, cry out to God in
> prayers and supplications not just for yourself and those
> who are close to you, but for all the earth?
>
> God, who was able to save Jesus from death, heard
> his prayer because of his reverence. God is able to save
> us from death; God hears us because of Jesus. Are we
> praying with reverence and living with fear of the Lord
> in our hour?
>
> Son though he was, Jesus learned obedience from
> his suffering. Do you promise to bend before God and
> learn obedience from your suffering, which is bound up
> with Jesus' pain and tears?
>
> Do you attempt to live in such a way that you do not
> cause needless suffering for others?
>
> When Jesus was made holy, he became the source
> of eternal salvation for all who obey him. Do you hand
> over your life to God, with Jesus, so that God can use
> you as a source of life and salvation for others?

This is our faith, this is our hope, and this is our comfort—
that Jesus suffered, prayed, obeyed, and died so that we
might live and die in God.

> *God, Father of Jesus and our Father, you are a God
> of life not of death. You have chosen us to know you in
> our hearts and to bring others closer to you. May we*

bear witness to the cross and resurrection of Jesus in our own lives. Let us go in peace to bring life to the world through our obedience to you. Amen.

Passion/Palm Sunday

From the Procession with Palms, Mark 11:1-10
Isaiah 50:4-7
Philippians 2:5-11
The Passion Account, Mark 14:1-15:47
or Mark 15:1-39

Jesus is on the edge of the city with the crowd that is approaching Jerusalem for the feast of Passover and the holy days that mark the liberation of the people from slavery in Egypt. It is a season that stirs up the hopes and frustrations of the people, who live now under the control of the Romans, whom they detest as not only their enemies but as enemies of God.

Jesus sends two of his disciples ahead with instructions to find a colt, untie it, and bring it back to him. If they are questioned, they are to give the word of Jesus as testimony to their actions. Obeying Jesus, they find the animal and return with it. The disciples put their cloaks on it, and Jesus sits on the colt. Others spread their cloaks on the road, and some people cut branches and reeds that they have brought from the local fields.

They go before Jesus and follow after him with cries: "Hosannah! Blessed is he who comes in the name of the Lord! Blessed be the reign of our father David to come! God save him from on high!" It is a crowd moved with high hopes, politically, socially, and religiously, all blurred together. This moment begins in triumph, with echoes of Abigail riding a colt to see King David and plead for mercy for her family and slaves.

Jesus enters the city of Jerusalem, the city of David, on the colt, pleading for mercy and salvation instead of just punishment for the people's breaking their covenant with God. The enthusiasm of the people is sincere, but many want a king to overthrow the Romans and erase their presence from the land. Theirs is a cry of vengeance, rage, and hatred as well as a cry of vindication. They would follow anyone who might wipe out the Romans and return the city and the nation to its former perceived glories. They are not faithful to God's hopes for them but only to their hopes for God. They are not followers of Jesus; they do not know faithfulness and the intimacy with God that Jesus tries to give them.

This is Holy Week. It is time to look at our lives and ask what Jesus asks of us this week. What does God need from us for others' salvation, for the glorifying of God in history? We need to ask ourselves before the headiness of this triumphal moment wears off what we are going to do to follow Jesus publicly this week and proclaim him as Lord. What "cloak" are we willing to spread before the Lord?

The verse before the gospel proclaims: "Christ became obedient for us, even to death, dying on a cross. Therefore God raised him on high and gave him a name above all other names." What name will you use to pray to God this week— Son of Man, crucified One, Lamb of God, Suffering Servant? And what are you willing to share with Jesus this week, as he suffers so that others may come to know him and be made new in life and hope this Easter?

The week begins. The cross looms. The crowd will quickly turn against him. Our best intentions will recede, our hearts will be frightened, and we will be tempted to run.

The readings from Passion/Palm Sunday are always the same: Isaiah 50:4-7 and Philippians 2:6-11. Only the gospel accounts change. Isaiah's song of the Suffering Servant, ever faithful, aptly describes Jesus. It should also describe us as followers of Jesus. Ours should be a well-trained tongue that speaks a word to the weary, a word that will rouse them, a word of hope, encouragement, healing, promise, and solidarity. Ours should be an ear that hears the word of the Lord faithfully day in and day out.

Jesus does not turn back, as many of us do so often. Instead he offers his back to those who beat him, his cheek to those who insult him. He does not shield his face from their buffets and spitting. He is vulnerable, open, defenseless, nonviolent. Jesus' help is from God, and he will not be disgraced. This is faithfulness, endurance, belief. He will be publicly humiliated and scorned, but God will not shame him. Even in torture and death Jesus will remain steadfast, trusting in God. He will become a holy sacrifice, a holocaust.

We are invited to follow Jesus to the cross with this kind of faithfulness. We believe that we are not alone, that Jesus has gone before us in faith. Nothing can stand against us or condemn us, for the mercy of God in the person of Jesus is with us as we walk the way of the cross.

We move from this description of the one who suffers because he is true to God into Psalm 22 and its refrain: "My God, my God, why have you abandoned me?" This reminds us of last week's reading from Hebrews: that Jesus learned obedience through suffering. His suffering was palpable, strong, terrible, emotionally and physically. His body was tortured and destroyed and his heart and soul unraveled before God.

It is a litany of what was done to Isaiah, to Jesus, and to many who still are tortured and brutally and legally destroyed at the hands of others. It is almost too hard to listen to, but we are to have an ear that listens to the word of the Lord. This brutality among humans is why God sought to gentle us. Jesus is scoffed at, mocked, made fun of, and God is mocked.

This is an insult to God. It recalls Matthew's gospel, with the Hinderer, Satan, saying, "If you are the Son of God, then God will not allow you to even stub your foot against a stone." This is baiting God, trying to define God in our terms, in Satan's terms, rather than loving God whether our lives are easy or not. Jesus is surrounded by evildoers, a mob. They have pierced his hands and feet in nailing him to the wood; he is stretched so taut that his bones stick out. He is naked and hung before the eyes of others, and he cries out to God not to be far from him, to be his help and hasten to aid him.

There is nothing left. The closing lines reveal that Jesus believes that God is close to him. He asserts that he will continue to proclaim the name of God to others. In the midst of the assembly he will praise God. In pain, he exhorts others to remember God and give glory to God, not to forget they are the people of the Holy One, with God's name inscribed on their hearts. Jesus does not forget; even in his tearing pain he reveres God, his Father.

The reading of Paul's letter to the Philippians is a proclamation of belief, hope, the life that we owe each other as baptized Christians. Our attitude is to be that of Christ, divine and human, but not grasping at divinity. Jesus emptied himself by becoming a slave, a condemned criminal, the most despised of us, dying on a cross.

We profess our faith. We witness with our lives this week that because of Jesus' obedience and service and unconditional love and mercy God has exalted him, raised him from the dead, and bestowed on him the name above all others—the name of God. All are called to bend and worship at the sound of that name. "Jesus Christ is Lord to the glory of God the Father!" With our lives, penance, almsgiving, fasting, rituals, liturgy, sacrifices, offerings, prayers, and supplications we proclaim in community the Lord of our lives: Jesus Christ. We glorify our Father by handing over our lives with Jesus. And we trust our offering will be accepted and made holy.

The journey draws near its close. The powers of darkness amass against Jesus, and he struggles to be faithful to his Father in the face of hatred, knowing that he is innocent. He remains merciful and forgiving. It is Palm/Passion Sunday. These are the last steps of the journey. We either follow in Jesus' bloody footsteps, or we find our way in the person of one or more of the characters of the passion narrative: the disciples who run away, the women who stay at a distance, Pilate, Judas, the high priest, those who stood at the cross and jeered him, or the centurion who says at the end, "Clearly this man was the Son of God!"

It is our moment, our hour of reckoning, our moment of truth-telling, our moment of being faithful to our baptism and freely walking with Jesus. We go down into his death so that we may rise with him in the waters of baptism and the light of the Easter candle and the breaking of the dawn, which heralds resurrection and the new creation.

The passion account is seen not only from the point of view of the disciples, but of the people who either believe in Jesus or betray him. Jesus asks Judas, 'What are you here for, friend?" He asks this of us as well. How do we want to walk and pray with Jesus this week? How do we want to walk with others? What are our feelings as we listen to the scripture readings? Can we too obediently accept even death, death on a cross? Can we speak words that will lift the weary and rouse our friends and fellow-disciples as we stumble after Jesus?

The passion according to Mark is the shortest, bluntest, and in some ways the most brutal of the passion accounts. If this man Jesus is who he claims to be—the Son of Man who will judge the nations with justice and come in glory with the power of God—then why did he die this way? And the underlying question: If we are his disciples, will we die this way? We recall the stories of the past weeks that resound with faithfulness, zeal for the house of God, obedience to no other power on earth but God's Law and Spirit, love unto death, mercy for enemies. The practice of these virtues will lead us to face darkness and injustice and the enmity of those who serve other gods and powers.

Death is a part of being human. We all must die. Jesus dies the way he lived, passionately devoted and obedient to God, and we are called to do the same. Life and death are to be a single sacrifice, a holocaust, a handing over completely of all we have and possess, including our lives, to God in sacrifice, in service, in obedience to the Law and the Spirit of the gospel. We are to spend our days in truth-telling, in mercy and forgiveness of others, and in single-hearted devotion to the Kingdom and the honor of God, in reverence and true worship. It is time to be destroyed so that God can raise us—the body of Christ—up again. It is time to head toward the place of sacrifice that God pointed out to Abraham, to the cross. It is time to be tested and revealed for who we really are: the children of God. It is time for the earth and all its creatures to know re-creation, grace and communion through the death and resurrection of Jesus

On the eve of the sabbath Pilate releases the corpse, and Jesus' body is placed in the tomb cut out of rock. It is over. Now the week of passion, of peace, of all life begins for us when we gather and the body is made whole, offered, sacrificed with Jesus. The Father will take us and raise us up in the power of the Spirit, and the resurrection will be seeded into the earth and all creation will sing for glory, made whole—holy—again. The covenant is renewed in our hearts, in our bodies, and made vulnerable to God throughout these days. The hour is upon us.

The following story is ancient, a Sufi tale from Iraq or Iran, heard from a friend during the Gulf War. It is called "One and a Half Followers."[2]

✛ Once upon a time there was a man who became the sultan of the Ottoman Empire. He was the leader of a vast and rich domain, a desert, hard to live in, but full of resources, beauty, and strength for those who know how to live there and learn to appreciate it. As soon as he was made sultan he was warned about one man, a caliph (a master teacher, like a rabbi) who, it was said, had thousands of followers. If he turned against the sultan his followers could overthrow him, and the caliph would become sultan himself. Or if the caliph sided with enemies outside the empire, the sultan wouldn't have a chance against the combined forces. But the sultan ignored all warnings. The years went by, and there were plots to overthrow the government, assassination attempts, coups that failed, and always the name of that one caliph was mentioned as being behind them all.

Finally the sultan heeded his advisors and sent for the man. He met him on the edge of the kingdom, near the desert, alone. The caliph came, riding out of the desert on his great Arabian horse. He got off in front of the sultan and knelt on the sand with his head touching the ground, as was the custom.

---

[2] I have used a version of this story in one of my earlier books, *Parables: The Arrows of God*, to illustrate the true meaning and reality of discipleship.

The sultan asked him one question: "Who is your master?"

The man rose, put his hand over his heart and said: "You are my master. Whatever I know of wisdom and truth in the desert, you taught me. Whatever I have of strength and power in the desert, you shared with me. You are my master. I will gladly give my life so that you may live."

The sultan embraced him warmly and said: "Good! I just wanted to make sure that you were still my follower. You know, all my advisors keep warning me about you and your hundreds of thousands of followers. They are afraid that you will turn them against me. But I know that you are my follower, and so all who follow you really follow me, whether they know it or not."

And they spoke amicably of their days together in the desert when they were young.

Finally, the sultan asked: "By the way, how many followers do you have?"

The caliph thought about it for a while and said: "One and a half, I think."

At this the sultan became furious: "What do you take me for, an idiot? Why would my advisors warn me about a man who has one and a half followers? I intend to find out just how many you do have."

And with that he had the caliph put in chains and threw him into prison.

The sultan then sent out a decree to his whole empire announcing that the caliph had fallen from grace and that he intended to kill him if all of his followers didn't show up on a certain day. Then he set up a tent on the edge of the desert. Inside it he stationed a dozen of his best soldiers and three of his best sheep. And he waited.

On the appointed day, he brought out the caliph in chains and they waited on the edge of the desert for the caliph's followers to appear. As the sun rose they came, on horseback, on camel, on donkey and ass, on foot and Arabian horse, hundreds of thousands of them, as far as the eye could see. The sultan looked at the caliph and said: "One and a half followers? Then who are all these people?"

The caliph answered: "I don't know, my Lord."

"We'll see," said the sultan.

The sultan faced the people and spoke: "This man, your master, has fallen from grace. I am going to behead him right now—and he drew his great scimitar—unless ten of you, his followers, are willing to give your lives so that your master might live."

There was a long, long silence. Then a man stepped forward, put his hand over his heart and spoke the ancient ritual: "Sultan, this man is my master. Everything I know of wisdom and truth, he taught me. Whatever I have of strength and power in the desert, he shared with me. I will gladly give my life so that my master may live."

The sultan snapped his fingers, the soldiers were summoned, they marched the man up to the tent, took him inside, dropped the flaps, then slit the throat of one of the sheep. The blood ran under the tent, across the sand dunes.

There was a terrible murmur in the crowd (and if you looked carefully, you could see people slipping away back into the desert—not a whole lot, but enough to notice). Then there was a long silence. The sun rose and the heat spread. The people started sweating from the masses of bodies, the sun, and the tension.

Then the sultan spoke again: "That's one. I need nine more, or your master dies."

Another murmur, then another even longer silence. Finally a woman stepped forward, and the crowd groaned. Even the sultan groaned, because she was a woman, and a woman only counts as one-half under Islamic law. But she put her hand on her heart and spoke the ancient words: "Sultan, this man is my master. Everything I know of wisdom and truth, he taught me. Whatever I have of strength and power in the desert, he shared with me. I will gladly give my life so that my master may live."

The Sultan snapped his fingers again and summoned the soldiers. They took her inside the tent, dropped the flaps, and slit the throat of another sheep. Once again the blood ran down the sand dunes under the tent. Pandemonium broke loose and all the people in the crowd scattered, running back into the desert as fast as they could. Soon there wasn't a soul left except the sultan and the caliph, who was still in chains.

The sultan set the caliph free and apologized: "I am sorry. You were right! You only have one and a half followers. How awful. You must feel terrible—all your work, your life and only one and a half followers!"

But the caliph looked at the sultan and replied: 'I know what you are thinking. You're thinking that the man is my one follower and the woman is half. But that is not true."

The sultan replied: "What do you mean? According to Islamic law, the woman is half, the man is one."

The caliph answered, "It has nothing to do with the law. It has to do with faithfulness and love. When the man stepped forward, he didn't know he was going to die. It could have been just a test. He's a good man, a bit arrogant, but he has possibilities. He is the half follower. When the woman stepped forward, however, she *knew* she was going to die. She is my one true follower!"

And when they tell this story they ask: Which one are you? Are you the one who is a bit arrogant but has possibilities? Or are you the one true follower, who knows that if you follow your master you will die with him? Or are you just one of the hundreds of people who *think* they are someone's followers?

We stand before the world today as a large mass of believers declaring our faithfulness, our promise to God. We will be known for who we really are, just as Jesus was revealed to be the Son of God, the Lamb of God, the Suffering Servant, the crucified One who goes before us.

Let us reflect on our faith, using an adaptation of today's reading from Philippians.

Do you believe that you must have the same mind and heart as Christ Jesus, who being in the form of God did not count equality with God something to be grasped at and so humbled himself even unto death?

Response: We do believe.

Do you believe that you need to humble yourself and become the servant of God and the servant of others, relying on Jesus' strength? (*We do believe.*)

Do you believe you are called to be obedient to God even to death, bearing your share of the sufferings of the cross, for others in the world? (*We do believe.*)

Do you believe that God highly exalted Jesus and bestowed on him the name by which we are saved? (*We do believe.*)

Do you believe in the name of Jesus, kneel only to his name, confess that only Jesus is the Lord of life, the Lord of history, the Lord of all the earth? (*We do believe.*)

Do you believe that Jesus Christ is Lord, to the glory of God the Father? (*We do believe.*)

This is our faith. This is our hope and salvation. We ask the strength of the Spirit of God as we follow the way of the cross this week with Jesus, who is Lord, to the glory of God the Father. Amen.

CYCLE C

The Crucified Lord

Introduction

The readings of cycle C focus on two realities: the holiness of God, and our glaring lack of virtue, which makes the theme of conversion an absolute necessity in our lives. It must be an ongoing conversion that sees God as God truly is and us as we truly are and acknowledges the gap that yawns between us. What bridges that gap is Jesus, the compassion and very holiness of God, who reaches out for us, insistently, never faltering in spite of our evil choices that stop the presence of God from healing and transforming the world.

The first readings deal with temptation and its corrective of preaching the good news of forgiveness and salvation expressed in one blunt word: Repent! Deuteronomy and Romans add that repentance is expressed in giving to God what belongs to God and emphasize that repentance encompasses mind, heart, and practice.

Luke's account of the transfiguration of Jesus in the presence of his friends positions Jesus as the center of all time and space, the heart of God's presence among us. "Listen to him" is the command that will carry us through Lent. In Genesis the promise of hope is sealed in sacrifice. The readings from Paul continue this theme, with the lure of heaven as our homeland. We have a choice: Do we live as enemies of the cross of Christ, or do we model the hope of Jesus?

The following three weeks train the eye of God straight at us, calling us to conversion, and always putting the reality of God's great mercy and forgiveness before us. There is an insistent cry, an immediacy, a demand in all the readings. *Now* is the time; we must not delay. We should grasp the hand of God now.

Exodus tells the harsh story of Pharaoh's refusal to let the people go forth to worship God alone. The reading begins with God hearing the cry of the oppressed people and send-

ing Moses to free them. God gives the divine name: "I Am."
Existence is holy. God *is*.

The reading from Corinthians smarts and burns. We could
end up like our ancestors who were sinners, who died in the
desert because they refused to acknowledge what God had
done for them. Jesus' words are harsh: "You will all come to
the same end unless you begin to reform"—a violent, unexpected end. It's time for us to bring forth fruit and not sap
energy from others by resisting the will of God. It is time to
repent.

Now comes hope. God removes our shame and brings the
people home and we are told with joy that we are a new
creation. We are the work of God. We are to be reconcilers,
ambassadors of Christ, with God appealing through and in
us. The gospel is the story of the lost son, the one who refuses to forgive, refuses to see the mercy, compassion, and
great love of his father, and refuses to celebrate and rejoice
over the return of the sinner. It is the story of those who
remain steeped in their own sin, their own cramped and angry world. It is about penance, reconciliation, eucharist, and
community. Where do we stand with the one who sits at table
with sinners?

The tension mounts in the week before the Passion but we
rejoice in the promise of God doing a new thing. The past
was glorious in what God had done, but, ah, now look! We
are being formed by God. We are to know only Christ and
the power flowing from his cross and resurrection. The story
from John tells of the woman brought before Jesus by people
intent on trapping him. It tells of those who will stop at nothing to demean Jesus, who are willing to destroy others in
their refusal to believe in and acknowledge the great mercy
of God. We are all sinners. Jesus will not condemn us, but he
will tell us the truth and stand against us in our sin and destruction of others.

This is the last straw. Now Jesus will be cast out and destroyed by people who refuse to ask forgiveness, to live as
reconcilers. Christ will make peace now only through the
blood of his cross, and we will be known either as his followers and friends or as his enemies. These readings are cries
for conversion. Lent is the springtime of our souls. Relent.

Repent. Remember. Resist. Repair the world. Refuse to be mastered by sin. Be reformed in the image of God, who is Jesus Christ the Lord.

Sunday of the First Week of Lent

Deuteronomy 26:4-10
Romans 10:8-13
Luke 4:1-13

Today's readings begin with offering to God in thanksgiving a portion of what we have been graciously given. The reading from Deuteronomy brings us back to our roots, reminds us that we are a nation that belongs to God, and recalls what our God has done for us. The story originates with God, who heard the cry of the people and brought them out of Egypt with power and signs and wonders and gave them land, a place to dwell in peace. Like our ancestors, God has given us sustenance, the fruits of the earth. In exchange we are expected to bow down in the presence of the Holy One and to take up a collection, a basket that is filled with offerings to the Lord. Then we are called to make merry over the good things that God has given to us.

This first reading of Lent calls us to imitate our God. We should first of all hear the cry of those who suffer unjustly and are persecuted, poor, and oppressed. We should take note of their afflictions, toil, and pain, and draw them forth with acts of justice, mercy, compassion, almsgiving, and solidarity. Then we can worship God and rejoice with them in what God has done for all of us. The season begins with a basket, a collection of offerings we make to God in thanksgiving for all God's gifts, especially Christ Jesus.

This season is universal. We are to worship, to tell the story, and to make it come true. Religious, economic, racial, and national groups are all to see that we honor and obey God first. Lent is the season to renew our baptismal commitments to God and to the community that publicly believes and worship God in obedience and gratitude. Sister Maria Augusta Rivas, a sister of the Good Shepherd who was killed in Peru in 1990, wrote just before she was murdered: "It seems that these might be the last days of my life: so I must take advantage of the time, which flies by so quickly. Otherwise I shall show up in eternity with empty hands." My grandmother used to say that we arrive in heaven only with what we have given away. Lent is a good time to start giving away in gratitude, sharing the riches we have been given.

Psalm 91 and its refrain—"Be with me, Lord, when I am in trouble"—remind us of our past history as slaves and our present as we face the testings of Lent and struggle to grow as believers in Jesus. The whole psalm is a prayer of trust, of security, of dwelling in the shelter of the Most High. It reminds us that we are protected by God's angels, that evil will not befall us, that with God we can tackle any violent and destructive situation. We are to cling to God and call upon God and we will be answered and delivered. The psalm also echoes the experience of Jesus in the desert with Satan, who uses the words to mock Jesus, trying to see if he really is the Son of God. But again, it is a comfort knowing that the angels have been given charge of us. We are not alone; we are guarded. They strengthen us and give us courage to face down the dragon and the lion, the asp and the viper. In the end, though, only the name of God delivers us.

Paul's Letter to the Romans continues this theme: "No one who believes in him will be put to shame." There is no basic difference among humans, no separation between Jew and Greek, young and old, rich and poor, Anglo and Hispanic and Native American and Asian and Black. God is rich in mercy toward all who call upon God's name. Everyone who calls on the name of the Lord will be saved.

God's mercy is offered to all of us together, not separately. We are all given gifts to help us through this season (and all of life), beginning with the gift of scripture, which is near to us, on our lips and in our hearts. The Word is Jesus Christ, the presence of God, crucified and raised from the dead by the Father, our Father who saves us. We are called to confession, to belief, to steadfast hope because we all have experienced the mercy of God. We are to call upon God, upon the name of Jesus the Lord, and we will be able to stand firm, to be secure, to persevere.

We are to rely on scripture and on the Word made flesh and to pray through and with this Word so that we remain faithful. The traditional disciplines of Lent are set forth in these opening readings: reading of the scriptures; prayer; almsgiving; fasting; avoidance of greed, insecurity, and fear; and acting with open hands and hearts toward others. Traditionally in this season we are to give to the poor as graciously as our God has given to us. This can take some practice.

The gospel message of the First Sunday of Lent is the same in every cycle, though from different traditions. This year's account of the temptations in the desert is from Luke's gospel. The setting is crucial. Immediately after his baptism, Jesus returns from the Jordan River bathed in the power of the Spirit. He is led by the Spirit into the desert to be tempted for forty days.

We too are led by the Spirit into the desert, and we will be tempted during these forty days, as Jesus was. But while the Spirit leads us, Jesus accompanies us. We are the sons and daughters of God—obedient, trusting, and worshiping God alone. We are here to find out how resistant we are to all that hinders the Kingdom of God and how steadfast we are in our continuing love of God.

The first temptation is always the same. When Jesus fasts, he grows hungry and the devil says to him, "If you are the Son of God, command this stone to turn into bread." The devil tempts Jesus to rely on his relationship with God to get what he wants and needs for survival. It is a temptation to selfishness. We too are tempted to focus our lives around our standard of living and to use our religion primarily to get God to take care of us, to break the usual order of creation to serve us first, and to use the powers of the Spirit for mundane things. After all, stones are meant for building homes, bridges, or roads, not for eating—and certainly not for weapons.

Jesus is clear about who he is. He does not need to prove it to the devil or anyone else. He will not bait God with his relationship. God knows his needs and Jesus trusts in God's care, quoting scripture back at the devil: "Not on bread alone do we live." Jesus' priorities are laid down early. He—and we—are to live on the word of God, on community, on eucharist. They are more important than our immediate needs. What makes us human, what makes us truly the children of God, is that we live on the Spirit as well as on food and drink. We live on friendship, love, discipleship, obedience, listening, and presence as well as bodily necessities. Jesus will teach that the community, the body of Christ, exists to sustain its members in fasting, almsgiving, prayer, penance, justice, and shared life.

The order of the second and third temptations in Luke's gospel is different from that of Matthew. In Luke's second temptation, Satan tempts Jesus by bringing him to a high place so that he can survey the world and see the powers of the world in motion: nations, governments, wars, power, greed, money, violence, nationalism, military might, pride. All these kingdoms are intent on only one thing: maintaining and expanding their power. It is interesting and sobering to realize that all these kingdoms belong to Satan, and he gives them to whom he wishes.

Jesus is clear that his Kingdom does not come in these ways. It comes through corporal and spiritual works of mercy, care for the poor, universal inclusion of others (even enemies and strangers), nonviolence, generosity, and compassion. Quoting scripture, Jesus says: "You shall do homage to the Lord your God; him alone shall you adore." Jesus lives under no sign of power; he lives under the sign of the cross, a sign of obedience, submission to being human, to living in a world that is human and yet subject to the power of the Spirit and God the Father. Jesus will preach and practice mercy, justice, healing, compassion, forgiveness, and welcoming of others in communion.

According to Luke, our second temptation is trying to use the powers of the world—economics, culture, organizations—to bring about the Kingdom of God. Instead, we should rely on God, even when God's methods do not appear to be pragmatic or effective.

The third and last temptation was probably the strongest and hardest to deal with in Luke's community. The devil takes Jesus up to the pinnacle of the Temple (the place of worship in the Jewish community) and tells him to throw himself down. If he is the Son of God and has a privileged relationship and closeness to God, then God will not allow him to be harmed.

Since time immemorial we have been tempted to use our relationship with God to save us from pain and suffering, even from death. But in Luke's gospel and Luke's community Jesus is the Suffering Servant of Isaiah, the prophet of the poor who defends God's name in the community in solidarity with the victims of injustice. Jesus judges justly on behalf of the earth's poor ones because he himself has been the victim of injustice, hatred, rage, and prejudice. He also has suffered at the hands of governments, religious groups, and even his own community, which betrays him.

Jesus makes it clear that while our relationship to God will not save us from pain, it does save us from inhumanity and from perpetuating violence on others. Such a relationship calls for us to stand with those who suffer and die unjustly, as Jesus stands with us in crucifixion and death, and then in resurrection.

These are the temptations of Jesus' life, and ours too. These are the temptations we will face head on as we accompany Jesus in the desert and decide whether to follow him to the cross and to eternal life. We seek not to test whether God loves us but to love God wholeheartedly and unconditionally; we are to remain faithful no matter what hardships may test us.

In the face of these temptations Jesus remains steadfast and the devil leaves him, but only for a while. Satan will await another opportunity—the opportunity that will culminate in the crucifixion, when his own disciples will fail their testing. It is Lent, and we are here to find out what we are made of. Can we rely on the power of the Spirit and remain faithful? It is a testing not just of individuals but of community. The world and its powers want to know where we stand. We pray that we stand together in the Spirit.

There is an ancient folktale told in many areas of Eastern Europe and India called "The Magic Pomegranate." It is a good story to look at today as we seek to give God the very substance of our life, as the first reading from Deuteronomy counsels us.

✢ Once upon a time there was a good king who had three sons. As he grew older he wondered which of his sons should inherit the responsibility of his kingdom, which son would be what his people needed when he died. Finally he called them in and told them that he wanted them to set off on a journey to see the world, to gain insight and wisdom and experience, and then to return to the kingdom after they had discovered something important or unique. The journey would test their education and preparation for their future in the kingdom.

The three brothers, who were close, were reluctant to go but obedient to their father. They decided, however, to come back early and share what they had found among themselves before appearing publicly in court. Off they went.

The first brother wandered north into the colder lands, following roads and well-known routes. He stopped in villages and marketplaces, listening, collecting tales and information. One day he was in a market looking at rugs. They were piled high in stacks, and he watched the owner sell a visitor a rug.

When the transaction was completed, the young man thought that he saw one of the rugs move! He went over and moved the others aside, and it happened again: the rug shimmered and rose just slightly off the ground! He looked at the owner, who was watching him, and they started bargaining. In due time the deal was made, and he owned a magic flying carpet, one that could take whoever was seated on it almost instantaneously to wherever the person wanted to go. The prince rolled it up and headed for home.

The second son wandered far to the west, using no maps. More adventurous, he was intrigued by new places, languages, and people. He traveled light and looked closely, long and hard. He went farther than anyone he had heard tell of, and he grew strong and hardy. The time slipped away quickly, and he knew he would have to begin his return journey so that he could meet his brothers on schedule.

He had begun to retrace his steps when he stopped one evening to get some food at an inn. Outside he watched a man looking at the stars through a long tube. He approached with fascination and interest. The man laughed and said he wasn't really looking at the stars, though what he saw was far away. He asked, "What would you like to see?" The young man replied, "A piece of my father's kingdom." The long tube was handed to him and immediately he saw in the small round orb the back garden of the palace where he had grown up. He recognized it in an instant. He must have the tube! The man was reluctant to part with it, but a deal was made. The second brother now had a magic telescope that could see anywhere the viewer wanted! He headed quickly for home.

The third brother wandered off to the southeast, winding his way back and forth, open to whatever. He watched and listened as he went into back alleys of towns, shacks along the river, through fields and small villages. He saw his father's kingdom in ways he had never noticed before, and he realized how different things and people were in a very small area. There were rich and poor, those who worked hard and others who didn't seem to make enough to feed their families. There were those who drove others to work for them but gave very little back, causing distress and frustration. There were sick and weak people who lived on the streets, enduring and desperate just for a piece of bread. There were others who had two or more houses and threw parties for their friends and fed leftovers to their dogs. He saw places of surpassing beauty: waterfalls, the sun setting into a barley field, the face of a young woman bent over her babe, the face of an old one whittling away on a piece of wood, making a toy for a child. The time slipped away for him too, and he headed for home with many ideas and feelings, but without anything tangible.

Just before he came to the palace he stopped to rest under a tree, and fell asleep. When he awoke the tree was in bloom with bright flowers and pomegranates. He reached up and picked one, admiring it, and promptly the tree disappeared. Now he had something, though he wasn't exactly sure what it was that he had!

Soon the brothers met and shared stories of their travels, delighted to be in each others' company again. At last they took out their treasures to share. The carpet, the telescope, and the pomegranate were passed around, examined, and wondered over. Then one of the brothers looked through the telescope and saw a far-off kingdom that was in mourning. He looked more closely and saw a king bent over the bedside of his only daughter. He was weeping as she slipped farther from him into the kingdom of death. "Look!" he declared to his brothers. "There is a kingdom and the king has offered wealth and his daughter's hand to anyone who can bring her back to him."

They looked at each other and smiled. They sat on the carpet and soon found themselves in the courtyard of the far kingdom. They were brought into the king's presence and said that they would try to bring his daughter back to him. The youngest son sat beside the young woman. He cut the pomegranate in half and slowly, carefully, fed the tiny pieces to her. With the first piece she stirred. The second brought color to her face. The third caused her breathing to steady and her heart to grow stronger. With the fourth her eyes opened, and she looked around her. She took the fifth piece, ate it, and sat up. Everyone rushed in rejoicing. The king embraced his daughter and turned to the brothers, "She is yours."

And they looked at each other. "Without my telescope you would not have known she was even here," said one. "Without my carpet we would never have been able to get here," said the other. "And without my pomegranate the princess would never have been saved," said the third.

Then the princess spoke. "I will decide whom I shall take in marriage, but first I want to ask each of you a question." She turned and spoke to the first one, "When you used your glass, did you lose anything?" "No," he replied. She asked the second, "Did you lose anything when you used your carpet?" "No," he replied. And to the last: "Did you lose anything when you used your pomegranate?" "Yes," he replied, "it is half gone." She smiled and said, "It is you I will marry, for you gave something you treasured but lost something of it in the giving. Such a gift is always richer and more of a gift."

And so she married the youngest son, who became a king in her father's land, and the other two brothers ruled together in their father's land.

What do we give? Each time we gather together we give to those in need for the sustaining of the community and the church, and we give our lives back to God. Our ritual is a way of life. Our public prayer is a way to hold each other accountable for our private lives. We then offer bread and wine, the firstfruits of our work and life together and as church. According to the ancient tradition of tithing, we are to give 10 percent of everything we make to God.

Sometimes it helps to look a bit more closely at what we give in relation to what we receive. How much do you give to the church and/or the poor in a week? What is 10 percent of your gross income for the week (remember to include unexpected income, gifts, and so on)? What's the difference between the two numbers? How do the results make you feel? Why? This kind of exercise enables us to get a glimpse of who we are really and where we stand before the world and God. What we give is returned a hundredfold. But often we don't know where it's given back—or who received it.

At the end of the offertory the priest says, "Pray with me, that our offering might be acceptable to God the almighty Father." This is the moment we hand over our lives and all we possess to God, so that God can transform our lives as powerfully as the bread and wine are transformed into the body and blood of Christ. We are the bread. We are the wine. We are the offering.

St. Ignatius Loyola, the founder of the Society of Jesus, composed a prayer that is central to those who follow him and Ignatian spirituality:

> Teach us, Lord, to serve you as you deserve;
> to give and not to count the cost;
> to fight and not to heed the wounds;
> to toil and not to seek for rest;
> to labor and not to ask for any reward, save that
>   of knowing that we do your will. Amen.

Prayed daily through Lent the prayer can help us to live not "on bread alone" but to be conscious of the needs of others and the wealth we have been given.

Many Native Americans in North America have a custom called potlatch, which is celebrated by an individual or a family in gratitude for all that the Great Spirit has given to them. They invite all their friends and relatives to feast with them, and they give the guests gifts. They give away their own possessions to those who need them or would like them as a symbol of gratitude for God's blessings. This is what the offering at Mass is: we give back to God the best of what God has given us, the firstfruits of all that we have.

The beginning of Lent is a good time to examine how we give individually and as a family, a community, a parish, a diocese, as friends together. It is also the time to look at what we give: time, money, resources, service, care for others, volunteer help, and so on. If we don't give daily, then there isn't much to celebrate and let God transform at the liturgy. This kind of giving is a privilege, an honor, and a blessing that is characterized by joy, because this is how God gives to all of us.

Lent is the season of resistance. Giving loosens the spirit so that the flesh can better resist. Traditional ways of resisting evil, Satan, violence, and sin are prayer, study, reading the scriptures, fasting, almsgiving, and penance. In this first week we need to ask ourselves what three things we are tempted to do in our lives that play into the hands of Satan; we should look at our weakest areas and choose three disciplines or traditional ways of resistance we will try to practice this Lent.

We end with a prayer service that begins with the *Asperges*, a sprinkling with water to remind us of our baptisms and the presence of the Spirit in the desert with us. In these prayers we ask God to make us what the world needs instead of asking God to do everything for us.

> Let us pray. Let us pray now for all the world and ask God for the courage and the strength to become what we offer—something that can become the bread and wine that the world needs now.

> For John Paul II and all those who lead us, that they will have the courage to speak out clearly on behalf of justice and that we will listen and take their words to heart, we pray to the Lord.

> *Response:* Lord, hear our prayer (or, Lord, spare your people).

> For the members of our church, that we might be an offering in spirit and in truth, in words and in deeds to God and to those in our community in need, we pray to the Lord. (*Response.*)

> For all those who are unemployed and living insecurely that we might be mindful of them and ease the burdens of their lives and those they are responsible for by helping them to get jobs and encouraging them with our good will and interest, we pray to the Lord. (*Response.*)

> For all those who are homeless and searching for a place to be accepted and belong, that they might find understanding and generosity as they struggle to survive, we pray to the Lord. (*Response.*)

> For all those who are ill, growing old, and facing death, that they might know many hours of comfort and hope

and delight in our presence with them and our care for them and their families, we pray to the Lord. (*Response.*)

For all our children, that they might look to us and see in us hope for the world and models to imitate in justice, hospitality, reconciliation, and peace, let us pray to the Lord. (*Response.*)

For all those who are excluded, blamed, kept at a distance, that they might remind us of God's disgust when we profess communion while separating one group from another, and that we may learn to welcome as God welcomes us all, we pray to the Lord. (*Response.*)

Father, you gave us your best gift, Jesus Christ your Son, our Lord, to be our savior, brother, and strength in food and drink and word. Let us trust in you and in one another and imitate Jesus' wholehearted giving of himself. Accept our gifts this Lent, accept us, all of us, and transform us into your body, the church in the world. We ask this in the name of Jesus Christ the Lord, through the power of the Holy Spirit. Amen.

Sunday of the Second Week of Lent

Genesis 15:5-12, 17-18
Philippians 3:17-4:1
Luke 9:28-36

We go back to our ancestor in faith, Abram, before his name was changed by God to Abraham as a sign of his encountering Yahweh God and being changed forever, before he was held in covenant with God and drawn into a relationship of faithfulness by God. It is a reading of unsurpassed hope, of promise for the future, of bringing forth a people who belong to God. We will be as numerous as the stars if we are credited with righteousness, as Abram was. The promise comes with land, a home that echoes the Kingdom of God here on earth.

The promise is sealed in sacrifice, the blood of heifers, goats, rams, turtledoves, and pigeons. It is done ritually, at dusk, splitting them in half. Then a smoking brazier and a flaming torch pass between the split pieces. The covenant is made. This land is given to the descendants of Abram—with boundaries. This covenant will grow into the giving of the Kingdom of God—with no boundaries. The covenant will be sealed with the sacrifice of God's own beloved Son.

It is interesting to note that God took Abram outside. God cannot be bound by walls. God begins by drawing Abram out past his dwelling place, past security, past whatever he thought he was or what he believed his future held. God is still breaking into our dreams, drawing us out, extending our horizons, and seeking to change our ideas of who we are and who God might be.

Our response to this covenant is Psalm 27, with its refrain: "The Lord is my light and my salvation." That light draws us past our fears. It is deep within us, and our hearts seek it always. We cry out for God's presence and believe that we will see the bounty of the Lord in the land of the living, even if it takes forever. In the meantime, we are to pray, live with courage, and wait, wait for the Lord. This proclamation is our reality. God is our hope, our resting place, our past and present and future.

Because God encompasses us as light, there is no room in our lives for fear. God has pity on us and hears us when we call. In return, we are called to listen and to seek God out. It is an attitude, a lifestyle, a discipline for all times. It is a way of praying.

Paul then seeks to remind the Philippians that they are first of all citizens of the Kingdom and that they dwell here waiting eagerly for the coming of Christ. We are not first citizens of the United States or Canada or any country but of the Kingdom of God, and we are to live accordingly. We are to imitate Paul and other believers who set an example by taking up the cross. Paul is discouraged by those who imitate the enemies of the cross of Christ. He finds himself repeating his warning again and again: Those who set their sights on the things of the world will end in disaster.

Paul cautions us: Are we enemies of the cross of Christ? Are we interested only in our own belly, our lifestyle, greed, possessions, power, money? Or are we citizens of heaven? Do we await with eagerness the coming of the Lord by practicing compassion, justice, sharing, thanksgiving? Do we live in hope of the resurrection begun in baptism in our flesh and in the world, and desire its completion when all things are subject to Jesus Christ? We are questioned, as in the temptation stories from last week, and we are encouraged to stand firm, knowing that there are others, like Paul, who love us and pray that we persevere in hope for a dearer life.

These readings are centered on the traditional gospel of this second Sunday of Lent, the account by Luke of the transfiguration on the mountain. It is a resurrection account that we can lean on in the weeks to come, as the powers of the world rise up violently against Jesus. We are called to choose where we stand in history, in belief, in practice, individually and in our communities.

Jesus takes Peter, James, and John—the leaders of his community, his friends, disciples, and relations—up a mountain, the usual place where sacrifices and promises and encounters with God take place in the history of the Jewish community. There they are given a vision (like Abram). While Jesus is praying, his face changes in appearance and his clothes become dazzlingly white. Two men, Moses and Elijah, are seen talking with him. This section of Luke and all of Lent are to be seen in the context of Jesus praying and our being invited to pray with him to God. All religion is to pray with Jesus to the Father, to gather all history, all the earth to God in the person of Jesus and transfigure it—let the power of the Spirit pass through it thoroughly and completely.

The two prophets—Moses, the lawgiver and liberator, and Elijah, the troubler of Israel—are speaking with Jesus of his passage, his death and resurrection. This is the focal point of all the promises of history and the future of the world, all that Jesus will fulfill in Jerusalem, all the sufferings and rejection, the fulfillment of sacrifice and worship.

But Peter and the others have fallen asleep, and when they awaken and see his glory, they do not understand. When Moses and Elijah leave, it is Peter, of course, who speaks immediately, ignorantly, to Jesus: "Master, how good it is for us to be here." True, but he really doesn't know what the presence of these figures means. He has heard the discussion of Jesus' passage, and so he glibly goes on: "Let us set up three booths, one for you, one for Moses, and one for Elijah." Peter has no idea of the power of Jesus, or who Jesus is; at best, Peter thinks he is another in the long tradition of the prophets and the teachers, the rabbis of the community. As he speaks, a cloud comes over them, as the cloud went before the Hebrews on their passage out of slavery and oppression through the desert of Sinai into hope and freedom. The cloud overshadows them, as the Spirit overshadowed Mary and brought the power of the prophetic spirit into her. Their fear grows as they enter the shadow, the cloud.

Then the voice from the cloud speaks: "This is my Son, my Chosen One. Listen to him." This is the proclamation of who Jesus is. It is the belief of Luke's community. The first and only response to knowing and seeing Jesus is to listen to him and to obey. We are not to have other ideas in mind—as Peter does, and we often do.

Then there is silence, and Jesus is alone in their presence. Finally, the disciples are also silenced; they are to tell no one what they saw. So they say nothing to anyone, but they probably talked a great deal to one another.

We do not understand the resurrection, the crucifixion, the life of the Spirit in behalf of the suffering and the poor, yet we too must speak to one another of these things. And we too must be silent in the presence of the power and awe of God in worship, in the proclamation of the gospel, and in the eucharist. This is our ritual covenant with God. In gratitude we grow in understanding. We awaken and see the glory of God in Jesus. This is the heart of our religion—to pray with

Jesus, to be silent, to listen, to see, and to grow in understanding of the mystery of Jesus at the center of all history and life and religion.

The mystery will be enacted in these next four weeks. Let us be still, listen, obey, and seek the face of God in the suffering of the earth, and so find ourselves close by this God hidden among us.

Thomas Merton wrote a short piece in *My Argument with the Gestapo* that turns us deep inside ourselves and questions where and who we are in the presence of the mystery of God among us, transfigured and seeking to transform us:

> If you want to identify me, ask me not where I live or what I like to eat, or how I comb my hair, but ask me what I think I am living for, in detail, and ask me what I think is keeping me from living fully for the thing I want to live for. Between these two answers you can determine the identity of any person. The better answer he has, the more of a person he is. . . . I am all the time trying to make out the answer as I go on living. I live out the answer to my two questions myself and the answer may not be complete, even when my life is ended I may go on working out the answer for a long time after my death, but at least it will be resolved, and there will be no further question, for with God's mercy, I shall possess not only the answer but the reality that the answer was about.

Lent is about identity, the identity of Jesus and the God that Jesus serves and obeys, the identity of the Spirit that drives Jesus in the world. It is also about our own identity. Are we obedient to Jesus' God and driven by that same Spirit? Or are we about another reality and the fabrication of our own identity apart from God, perhaps regarding God as just one of many factors in our construction.

Peter, James, John, and all the disciples are drawn into the mystery of Jesus in the Father through the Spirit, and they are slow to perceive and understand, as most of us are. They have their own agendas and hopes for Jesus, as we have ours. We all must be led up the mountain to the place that gives us larger horizons and deeper hearts, so that we can be lured into the holy Mystery that is God come among us in the Word and in the Spirit. Unless we concentrate on finding God, on letting ourselves be overshadowed by the cloud, and on listening to the Word, we will blunder about like Peter, working on our own building plans, oblivious of whose presence we are in and who seeks to draw us into friendship with God.

There is a teaching story called "Needle in a Haystack" that recalls us to our priorities, as Jesus sought to bring his friends up the mountain to see him as he truly was, with his hidden glory streaming through.

✢ Once upon a time some students were looking for God. But they couldn't seem to find God. They studied, they took courses with the best teachers—and some who weren't so good. They traveled, kept silent, and watched. They listened to the old for wisdom. They experimented with the ancient disciplines of many religions, for they seemed to overlap in this area of finding the Holy One.

Finally they came to their current teacher, who was a great preacher, and announced that looking for God in the world was like trying to find a needle in a haystack. "Exactly!" the teacher exclaimed. "If you know how to find a needle in a haystack, you'll know exactly how to find God in the world. Go home, and for your homework figure out how you'd look for a needle in a haystack.'

Off they went, moaning and groaning. The next morning they all came in, some with answers, some not. Some had tried very scientific routes; some had dreamed an answer or imagined one; some had given up, thinking it was an impossible task, especially to do overnight.

"What have you learned," the teacher asked.

The first answer came: "I'd burn down the haystack."

"Very good! That is the way of total renunciation, giving up all for the one, but I think there are really very few people in the world who are that committed, that obsessed with finding God. Besides, it seems a shame to waste all the hay. It doesn't seem a very good use of the gifts we have been given and of others' hard work."

He turned to the rest of them: "Any other ideas?"

A woman spoke up: "A needle feels different from hay. I would sit and sift through all the hay, day and night, until I found the needle. It would take a while, or I might get lucky, but I'd find it eventually."

"Very good," said the teacher, "that is the way of experience and knowledge, but it takes a good deal of patience. It helps if you live long enough so that you can sift through your life experiences, mistakes, relationships, unexpected encounters, and history itself so that you can find that needle. Any other ideas?"

Another student spoke up: "I'd get a group of people together to find it. We'd be organized and efficient."

"Good," said the teacher. "That's working together. But who gets to keep it once someone has found it? And how would the others feel when they had worked so hard and another found it? Would it be passed on to them eventually? Any other ideas?"

A voice yelled out: "I'd just jump into the haystack, and with my luck, I'd get stuck by the one needle hidden there!"

Everyone laughed, and the teacher replied: "True, but then you'd associate finding God with pain. And some people can jump in a haystack all their life and never find the needle."

They were all silent. Finally the teacher spoke again: "It's so easy. All you need is a magnet. Tie a magnet on a string and walk around the haystack. Follow the slightest quiver of movement in the magnet, and it will lead you straight to the needle. In fact, what you can't perceive is that with each quiver and movement of the magnet, the needle is quivering too. It is waiting for and looking for the magnet to come closer and closer. When the magnet draws near, the needle will leap out of the hay and onto the magnet. When you have a magnet looking for God, God quivers when you come close and then jumps right into your arms!"

They were stunned. The silence deepened.

Then he spoke again: "What do you use for your magnet?"

For Christians the answer is simple. We use the scriptures to find God in our lives and in our history and world today. We delve into today's text, into the vision of the transfiguration and the discussion among Elijah, Moses, and Jesus with the three disciples watching and listening in the presence of God the Father. The easiest and truest way to use our "magnet" is with others (as Jesus invited Peter, James, and John up the mountain with him). It is truer still in the context of preaching and being held accountable for what we hear. Then, afterward, we can stand on our words and become what we have professed. We go out into the world and become the words that the world needs to hear in its search for God.

A good homily, scripture study, or prayer is a mixture of the people, the text, the preacher, and the presence of the Word in our midst. As we listen and share what we have heard and believe, others are also fed and, in turn, they feed us with their portion and belief and understanding. Like the disciples, we need to talk to one another before we go into the world. We need to share what it is that we profess to believe about Jesus, the Father, and the Spirit, about the cross and resurrection in Jesus' life, in history, and in our own lives.

There is another way to look at the scriptures and our coming to understand and believe. It is a story from the early Fathers of the Church that stirs up some questions.

✛ Once upon a time a student asked her master, "What is the difference between one who has wisdom and knowledge and someone who is enlightened?"

The teacher immediately responded: "Easy. The one who has wisdom and knowledge is the one who carries a candle in the darkness and lights the way. The one who is enlightened is the one who has become the Torch itself."

Then she eyed the student carefully and asked, "Which are you trying to become?"

Oftentimes we are intent on gaining the wisdom, knowledge, and the insight that will enable us to cope with our lives and give us some direction or immediate meaning. By our baptisms we have been entrusted with the Light, the word of the scriptures. We are to bring it to the Kingdom intact and burning brightly.

If only Peter and the others had been awake and aware of what was going on! They missed the moment. They had other things and thoughts on their minds and they had another image of who Jesus was for them and history. Today is a day of dreams and visions, and yet laced throughout those visions is the hardest reality of all: the cross. We ritually enact it and seek to be drawn more deeply into Jesus' passage each Lent, each Holy Week and during the Easter Vigil, but it is the mystery of our entire lives together. It is a communal ritual and a communal life. Today we are to look at the cross and our passage through life and death to resurrection, our embracing of the cross and what that means for us and our friends and relatives, and for history.

As church, the body of Christ, we reveal God's glory to others when we practice the traditions of the Law and the prophets and imitate Jesus' way in the world. Four primary practices are denouncing injustice and evil in the world, obeying the Spirit of the laws of the scriptures and the church, celebrating eucharist and becoming communion, and revealing the power of God present in suffering. We are called to be true friends and lovers of the cross of Christ, or we are revealed to be enemies of the cross of Christ.

The cross is the core of our belief, the core of our struggle to be true as disciples, and the core of Jesus' message. We have been told, "If you wish to be my disciples, then begin by denying your very self, picking up your cross and coming after me" (Mark 8:34). We shudder just to hear the words directed to us.

What is the cross? Often we think in terms of our cross, but our small pains and fears are splinters at best, often results of what we ourselves have done, or our weaknesses and failures, or just the usual course of sickness, aging, or the limits of being human. The cross was and is a public reality, a destruction of human beings, one at a time, legal, benefiting others, instilling fear and hate, drawn out, and used specially by one group with power over others. It was brutal, inhuman, insensitive. It forced the one being executed to participate in his own destruction by carrying the cross. It was and is based on a culture of death, violence, and hatred.

What does the cross look like today in the world? Perhaps we should look at some statements of the church, which sees the cross as a looming reality in the world.

We all know well that the areas of misery and hunger on our globe could have been made fertile in a short time, if the gigantic investments for armaments at the service of war and destruction had been changed into investments for food at the service of life (John Paul I, *Redemptor Hominis*, 1979).

Action on behalf of justice and participation in the transformation of the world fully appear to us as a constitutive dimension of the preaching of the Gospel, or, in other words, of the church's mission for the redemption of the human race and its liberation from every oppressive situation (Synod of Bishops, *Justice in the World*, 1971).

Injustice reigns when the laws of economic growth and ever greater profit determine social relations, leaving in poverty and destitution those that have only the work of their hands to offer. Being aware of such situations, the church will not hesitate to take up the cause of the poor and to become the voice of those who are not listened to when they speak up, not to demand charity, but to ask for justice (John Paul II, the Philippines, 1981).

It is not enough to recall principles, state intentions, point to crying injustices and utter prophetic denunciations; these words will lack real weight unless they are accompanied for each individual by a livelier awareness of personal responsibility and by effective action. It is too easy to throw back on others responsibility for injustices, if at the same time one does not realize how each one shares in it personally (Paul VI, *Octogesima Adveniens*, 1971).

The fundamental moral criterion for all economic decisions, politics, and institutions is this: They must be at the service of all people, especially the poor.

As individuals and as a nation, therefore, we are called to make a fundamental "option for the poor." The obligation to evaluate social and economic activity from the viewpoint of the poor and the powerless arises from the radical command to love one's neighbor as one's self. Those who are marginalized and whose rights are denied have privileged claims if society is to provide justice for all (*Economic Justice for All: Pastoral Letter on Catholic Social Teaching and the U.S. Economy,* United States Conference of Bishops, 1986).

These statements call us to penance, almsgiving, and fasting. These traditional practices of Lent call us to look at the cross. The cross is born of injustice, sin, and evil, and we are all guilty of collusion with evil that is systematic, calculated for the gain of others, violent in method and outcome. Penance begins with our acknowledgment of sin, a confession on our lips, and a firm purpose not only not to engage in such actions again, but to atone for and seek to repair the damage that has already been done. Penance unites us with the victims of injustice and reminds us of the closeness of the body of Christ. We are exhorted in this season to do penance and to undo evil structures, laws, and institutions that are unjust.

We each have a share in the cross, the burdens that history and the world lay on other human beings. Each of us is called to accept our share of the burden by doing penance for our own sin and collusion with evil, as well as doing penance for the larger evils of the world in which we all participate, whether we are aware of them or not. This is the cross. Jesus' passage and our passage are about dragging the sin, evil, and horrors of the world to Calvary and crucifying such inhumanity. As we do this, we uncrucify those who suffer because of our refusal and the world's refusal to believe and to see Jesus as Son of Man, Son of Justice, and Lamb of God.

This Sunday is a day of dreams and miracles. Joao Bosco Burnier, a Jesuit killed while going to the aid of a tortured woman in Mato Grosso, Brazil, wrote in a letter to Cardinal Arns: "In this world of fear and force, it will be a miracle if justice triumphs in the end: but miracles do exist."

Sunday of the Third Week of Lent

Exodus 3:1-8, 13-15
1 Corinthians 10:1-6, 10-12
Luke 13:1-9

This is the day of the First Scrutiny for catechumens, and it is a day of warnings to those who call themselves believers, Christians. Watch out! The tradition tells us that all that has happened before serves as a warning and as an example to us. If you think you are standing upright, watch out lest you fall! We are to reform our lives, for we who have been baptized, confirmed, and given eucharist and forgiveness have an ever greater obligation to be faithful to our baptisms.

The readings begin with the call of Moses, who lives in exile after being condemned to death in Egypt for killing an overseer in a blind rage. Raised as a highborn in Egypt, Moses is now an Israelite who tends the flock of his father-in-law. In the desert the presence of God appears to him in a bush that burns but is not consumed. The Lord sees him coming and calls out to him from the bush, "Moses, Moses!"

He answers, "Here I am!"

God speaks plainly, "Come no nearer and remove the sandals from your feet, this is holy ground." God announces that he is the God of his father, of Abraham, of Isaac, and of Jacob, and Moses hides his face, afraid to look at God. This is the God of the early covenant, the God to be feared. The person who sees God will die. This is the God to whom we owe our very existence, all we possess. We live to honor and worship and sacrifice our lives in obedience to God's will.

God wants Moses to do something. God has heard the cries of the chosen people, now victims of injustice, and God intends to send Moses to rescue them and lead them out of bondage in Egypt into a land flowing with milk and honey. Their salvation—all salvation—means freedom, hope, a life of dignity and promise in the future, especially for those denied their humanity and life by others.

But Moses is hesitant. He questions God, "What shall I say is your name?"

God replies, "I am who am."

"I am"—all existence, ungraspable, mystery, all that is and will be, life, hope, creation unfolding, holiness, completeness. In other words, don't ask, because God cannot be contained in a simple word or name.

"I AM sent me to you" is what Moses is to answer. He is called to a new life, sent to those in bondage.

God sends Moses to the people. God is theirs, and they are God's, for all generations. We are also called forth by God to be sent to others. If we worship God, we hear the cry of the suffering and afflicted, those who are the victims of the powers of this world. If we worship God, who cannot abide injustice and needless pain, we obey God's command to set others free and share our life with them. We know holy ground in the presence of Jesus, in the eucharist, in the word, and in the flesh of every human being, especially those broken and torn.

God's work is always about witnessing the suffering of all God's people and rescuing them by means of those sent to earth in God's name: "I AM who I am," Yahweh, or, as the Jews spell it without vowels in the Torah, for the name of God should not be written, YHWH. What does this name mean to you? Do you dwell in the land of milk and honey now? What is it like? Has God sent you to do anything? What? How? What do you tell people about your God?

Human life hasn't changed much since the time of Moses or Jesus: there are simply different groups of people who are oppressed and denigrated. Listen to the words of *Gaudium et Spes* from the Second Vatican Council:

We are at a moment in history when the development of economic life could diminish social inequalities if that

development were guided and coordinated in a reasonable and human way. Yet all too often it serves only to
intensify the inequalities. In some places it even results
in a decline in the social status of the weak and in con-
tempt for the poor. While an enormous mass of people
still lack the absolute necessities of life, some, even in
less advanced countries, live sumptuously or squander
wealth. Luxury and misery rub shoulders (no. 63).

This is what Moses was sent to change. This is what *we*
are called to change. God cannot abide inequality and in-
flicted pain, especially when it is done by those who claim to
be believers.

The refrain of the psalm echoes God's care: "The Lord is
kind and merciful" (Psalm 103). Because of who God is, we
must praise and bless God and seek with all our being to
remember God's benefits and sing God's praises. God par-
dons our iniquities, heals our ills, redeems our life from destruction, and then crowns us with kindness and compassion. But God is also just. As God made known the ways of
justice to Moses and all the children of Israel, the story continues in the deeds done in Jesus on our behalf. God is merciful, slow to anger, gracious, abounding in kindness. To be
the recipient of that kindness all we must do is fear God—
not a groveling, debilitating fear, but the healthy fear that is
the source of awe and wonder at the sheer holiness of God,
who lets us approach nearer and nearer and nearer.

But lest we think we are ready to obey and be sent like
Moses, and lest we fail to see ourselves among those who
destroy life and seek to enslave creation and other human
beings, Paul's first letter to the Corinthians brings us up short.
I want you to remember this: our fathers were all under the
cloud and all passed through the sea; by the cloud and the
sea all of them were baptized into Moses. All ate the same
spiritual food. All drank the same spiritual drink (they drank
from the spiritual rock that was following them, and the rock
was Christ), yet we know that God was not pleased with most
of them, for "they were struck down in the desert."

Practically the entire generation that left Egypt perished
in the desert, wandering while the people slowly and pain-

fully learned to be faithful, to listen to God, and to obey Moses and the Ten Commandments. It was primarily their children who were to enter the land of milk and honey. And they too had to learn—again and again and again.

Paul wants us to remember our history and apply it. We all have read and listened to the same word and shared the same eucharist, sacraments, community, Spirit. Is God pleased with most of us? The history of God's people is an example for us, a warning. We are not to take for granted what has been given. Do we belong to God? Do we move forward, faces toward the Kingdom of God, toward the true worship of God? Are we standing upright? Or are we about to fall? Or have we fallen already? We must rely on God alone and the presence of God revealed in Jesus and the word.

What about our wicked desires? What about our grumbling? Some of the people were killed by the destroying angel. It seems this angel serves God and executes judgment on those who refuse to be converted, to obey. Will our lives one day be used as a warning for the next generations? Will they know exactly what the prophet and the preacher is referring to?

The reading from the gospel of Luke follows in this vein. It is a brutal account, echoing Paul's words. It is a warning, an examination of conscience, and a chance to choose where we stand and what we think we are according to God's criteria. Luke tells of those who bring a story to Jesus about Galileans who were sacrificing to God; Pilate had mixed their blood with their sacrifices and destroyed them. Jesus refers to what all the people were thinking, that God punished them because of their sin. Then Jesus adds another reference familiar to all, the story of the eighteen whose blood was spilled when a tower fell on them. He asks those around listening to him: "Do you think that these Galileans were the greatest sinners in Galilee just because they suffered this?" And Jesus answers his own question: "By no means! But I tell you, you will all come to the same end unless you reform!" This is the prophet of God exhorting the people to conversion, to radical change, to turn back toward God and away from their usual way of life.

These are stories of death, similar to those that fill our newspapers and television screens today. We see the stricken faces of children, firefighters, parents, witnesses; their grief is so closely observed that it is embarrassing to watch. Some disasters are natural but many are the handiwork of humans, of nationalistic wars, of ancient feuds dug up and set in motion once again. We blame others across borders for our troubles and decisions, but the results come home to roost. Or, as the people on the streets in our cities say, "The war has come home."

Jesus uses destructive events to say something about God. His message is not that God is doing this, but that others are, and that this is the result of sin and evil. God is always urging us to come back, to reform. Jesus continues with a parable.

A man had a fig tree growing in his vineyard and he came out looking for fruit on it but did not find any. He said to the vinedresser: "Look here! For three years now I have come in search of fruit on this fig tree and found none. Cut it down. Why should it clutter up the ground?" In answer the man said, "Sir, leave it another year while I hoe around it, and manure it; then perhaps it will bear fruit. If not, it shall be cut down."

There are some odd things in the parable (of course!). What's a fig tree doing in a vineyard? Was it there before the vines were planted and just allowed to stay? A fig tree takes about seven years to bear fruit, so it isn't surprising that there is no fruit after three years. Has Jesus' ministry and teaching been going on for three years? Is he expecting some sort of fruit from those who were there before he came to plant the vineyard that produces every year? The judgment is to cut the tree down if there is no fruit, no life, no future. In Jesus' Kingdom and community is there always a year of favor from the Lord? Are we to bear fruit in every season, every year, even in times of drought, even in the desert? And who is the vinedresser? Will Jesus or the community of his disciples always seek to save even one lone fig tree that isn't producing, that hasn't heard, that hasn't taken the message to heart, repented, and changed? After all, it's halfway through Lent now! Where are we? What kind of fruit have we been producing? Any at all? After all these years since our baptism, years of confirmation, eucharist, reconciliation, scripture, and prayer, does God have anything at all to show for our life in the Spirit? Or is it time for some serious fertilizing and hoeing? Will any of us bear fruit this year?

Fig trees and vineyards are images of peace because they indicate long periods of time without war or local squabbling and fighting—each person under his or her own fig tree, feeding future generations and drinking of the wine of the Spirit, the promise of God's goodness in the land. All is at peace in this image. What is our world like these days? Where does it need fertilizing and hoeing? Are we, like Moses, being sent by God to do that hoeing and fertilizing? Or are we sinners in desperate need of reform ourselves? Will we come to a bloody, violent end, caught in the evil and the powers of the world? Are the world's victims—like Jesus and the prophets and his true disciples—the ones bearing fruit? Remember: "Unless the seed falls into the ground and dies, no fruit comes forth." Are we dying to ourselves? Are we standing in solidarity with the right folks?

All these questions can be devastating, paralyzing, frightening, but they are also necessary. Far too often we take our status in the Kingdom too lightly, oblivious to the pain and injustice of the world and to our own lack of engagement with the forces of resistance and prayer and penance. The church in her better moments, more prophetic moments, concurs with the words and heart of Jesus. Listen to the words of the U.S. Catholic bishops expressed in *The Challenge of Peace* (1983):

> It is clear today, perhaps more than in previous generations, that convinced Christians are a minority in nearly every country of the world—including nominally Christian and Catholic nations. In our own country we are coming to a fuller awareness that a response to the call of Jesus is both personal and demanding. As believers we can identify rather easily with the early church as a company of witnesses engaged in a difficult mission.

To be disciples of Jesus requires that we continually go beyond where we are now. To obey the call of Jesus means separating ourselves from all attachments and affiliation that could prevent us from hearing and following our authentic vocation. To set out on the road to discipleship is to dispose oneself for a share in the cross (cf. John 16:20). To be a Christian, according to the New Testament, is not simply to believe with one's mind, but also to become a doer of the word, a wayfarer with and a witness to Jesus. This means, of course that we never expect complete success within history and that we must regard as normal even the path of persecution and the possibility of martyrdom (no. 276).

But the remedy is in sight: fertilizing and hoeing. Toward the very end of the text the pastoral letter speaks about how to live in a world of violence, hatred, and denial of other human beings as the body of Christ, even for those within the community of believers:

Prayer by itself is incomplete without penance. Penance directs us toward our goal of putting on the attitudes of Jesus himself. Because we are all capable of violence, we are never totally conformed to Christ and are always in need of conversion. . . . We call upon our people voluntarily to do penance on Fridays by eating less food and by abstaining from meat. . . . Every Friday should be a day significantly devoted to prayer, penance and almsgiving for peace.

It is to such forms of penance and conversion that the Scriptures summon us. . . .

The present nuclear arms race has distracted us from the words of the prophets, has turned us from peacemaking, and has focused our attention on a nuclear buildup leading to annihilation. We are called to turn back from this evil of total destruction and turn instead to prayer and penance toward God, toward our neighbor, and toward the building of a peaceful world. . . .

Parents who consciously discuss issues of justice in the home and who strive to help children solve corflicts through non-violent methods enable their children to grow up as peacemakers. . . .

To youth: We call you to choose your future work and professions carefully. How you spend the rest of your lives will determine, in large part, whether there will any longer be a world as we know it. We ask you to study carefully the teachings of the Church and the demands of the gospel about war and peace (nos. 297-307).

We need to do the work of God, the work to which we are called as followers of Jesus. We need to know to whom we belong. A story is in order. This one, from the oral tradition of Turkey, is called "The Magic Sandals of Abu Kassim."

✛   Once upon a time there was a Jew named Abu Kassim. He made his living by selling rags, and although he worked hard, luck was against him and he was very poor. Every morning Abu Kassim would walk along the street, calling: "Rags for sale, rags for sale. Come and buy my rags." But no one wanted them, and soon Abu Kassim grew so poor that he had only one torn shirt, one ragged pair of pants, and no shoes at all.

One day, after he had been walking all morning, he sat down by the side of the road to rest. He opened the small sack his wife had given him and took out a piece of crusty bread for his lunch. As he did, he noticed an old man with a long white beard coming toward him, looking tired indeed. "Good day, Grandfather," he said.

"Good day," answered the old man.

"Please," said Abu Kassim, "you look so tired, won't you sit beside me and rest?" Then Abu Kassim held out his piece of bread. "Here, take this," he said. "You must be hungry. I wish I had more to offer you, but this is all I have."

The old man thankfully accepted the bread of Abu Kassim and ate it slowly. He didn't waste a single crumb. When he had finished, he turned to Abu Kassim and spoke: "You have a kind heart, and I have the power to grant you a special wish. Ask for anything you want, and it shall be yours."

Abu Kassim was startled, "Oh, if only I had a pair of shoes," he sighed. At once, as if by magic, the man drew out of Abu Kassim's sack of rags a pair of shiny new sandals. "Thank you, thank you," Abu Kassim cried in disbelief. Without delay he put on his new shoes. How comfortable they were! How quickly Abu Kassim could walk in them! He knew at once they were the most wonderful sandals he had ever had or could ever hope to have. He turned to thank the old man, but the old man was gone.

From the very moment that Abu Kassim put on those sandals, his luck began to change. Soon he was walking more quickly than ever, calling out his wares, and more people bought them. He was taking home gold coins every day. Before long he opened a shop. Now he sold hats, pants, shirts, and skirts, and he charged prices so low that even the poorest could afford them. People came to his shop from all corners of the city.

Months passed, then years. Abu Kassim breathed easier. He built a house and had good clothes and ate good food. And he always remembered to share the bulk of what he made with the poor. All this time, Abu Kassim wore his sandals. But as time went on, they began to wear out. There was a hole here, a tear here, a creak here, a squeak there, a rip here, a crack there. One day as he was walking a neighbor said to him: "What a fine shirt you have, what fine pants you have, even an embroidered cap—but, for shame, look at your ragged shoes! What a disgrace." He looked at his sandals, and was ashamed. My neighbor is right, he thought. I must get rid of these shabby sandals, but how?

The next day Abu Kassim went to a shoe shop and bought a pair of new sandals and put them on. On the way home, he threw his old sandals in the river. He watched them sink, happy to be rid of them.

The very next morning, two fishermen appeared at his door. "Abu Kassim, look what we found in our nets!"

They held out his sandals, dripping and wet. Oh, no, he thought to himself. He thanked them politely and sent them away. How was he to get rid of them?

He went to the bath house with his sandals tucked under his arm. And he left them there, thinking someone would pick them up. The next morning, though, a small boy appeared at his house with the sandals: "Look, you must have forgotten and left your sandals at the bath house." Oh, no, he thought again, but politely he thanked the boy. Now he was getting desperate. Finally, he had an idea.

He waited until the sun set and the sky grew dark. Then he took a shovel and went to a big field and dug a hole. He buried the sandals so deep that he was sure no one would find them. He smiled. He'd gotten rid of them at long last. But the very next morning who should appear at his door but soldiers, looking stern. "Abu Kassim," they said, "last night someone saw you burying a treasure in a field. That land belongs to the Sultan, so any treasure there belongs to him. You must dig it up and give it to the Sultan, at once."

Abu Kassim laughed and led the soldiers to the treasure. They dug it up, and when they saw the sandals and he told them the story, they laughed too.

Abu Kassim thought to himself: these sandals and I cannot be parted from each other. He shook the dirt from the sandals and put them back on. They were as comfortable as ever. With them, he walked ever more easily than before. "My dear sandals," he said. "I do not know what I did to deserve you, but you are certainly the best present I have ever been given." Then Abu Kassim remembered the old man and knew who he was. He was Elijah the prophet, sent by God to help the Jews when they are in need.

Abu Kassim wore those sandals for as long as he lived, for no matter how many holes, rips, and cracks they had, no matter how many creaks and squeaks they developed, those sandals never wore out. Abu Kassim grew in wisdom and generosity and good friends. Hope stayed with him all his days, in spite of changes in luck and life.

Everyone knew him by his sandals. He belonged to the one who sent the gift—he belonged to those sandals.[1]

We must look at pain and evil and those who suffer, and we must remember that we are responsible for our brothers and sisters. We must carry them in our hearts and hold them dear. If we forget, the tide of evil rises to engulf us all due to our selfishness, fear, insecurity, anger, and violence. God is always trying to get us to come nearer, even if God is found most clearly in those who are bloodied and forgotten.

Before he was murdered, Jesuit Ignacio Ellacuría worked in barrio parishes and in the fields in El Salvador documenting human-rights abuses. One of the massacres that he wrote passionately about was in the village of Mozote, in Morazan, El Salvador, in 1981. He called the victims the anonymous martyrs of Mozote.

This crucified people is the historical continuation of the servant of Yahweh, the one from whom the sin of the world continues to strip all human features, from whom the powers of this world continue to steal all— taking everything—even life itself, above all life.

The crucified people are there. Sometimes we see them on television, but in reality they don't get much of our attention. They are not known. Everything is done to hide them so that our western and bourgeois tranquility is not disturbed.

Anything is more important than to really hear the voice of God that, with indescribable moans or loud cries, calls us to see the open wounds of universal injustice.

It is possible that some feel that presence too obscure or that voice too far away and weak. These poor souls! They are so far from God. And those who crucify constitute the beast of the Apocalypse. And those who

---

[1] I have told this story often from notes on a piece of paper, but I have no idea where I got it. Forgive me, but if the teller has been forgotten, the story certainly hasn't.

make themselves deaf and blind, because to them this does not seem to be a religious problem, they are the lukewarm whom God, disgusted, has spit out of his mouth.

What are we to do? We are to repent, reform, change, be converted. We must listen and feel with God the agony of those who suffer. And then, we are to do penance, fast, give alms, and work mightily for justice. In all things, daily, we must seek, as Etty Hillesum puts it, to "safeguard this little piece of God in ourselves." And in all of God's children.

Sunday of the Fourth Week of Lent

Joshua 5:9, 10-12
2 Corinthians 5:17-21
Luke 15:1-3, 11-32

This is Laetare Sunday, a time for rejoicing. Lent is more than half over, and redemption and forgiveness and new life draw closer to us. Today we look to God, who has "removed the reproach of Egypt [slavery]" from us and who has made us a "new creation." Now all is new! God does not hold our transgressions against us (the story of the lost son) but reconciles us to himself and then graciously gives us the message of reconciliation to give to others. We are made ambassadors for Christ. Christ has died so that we might become the very holiness of God. We will be reminded of our baptisms, of "putting on" Christ with our white garments. This is also the Sunday when the catechumens experience the Second Scrutiny, reminding them—and us—of the mercy and forgiveness of God.

In the first reading the Lord speaks to Joshua, the leader chosen to follow Moses. The people are entering the promised land and learning what it means to live together as witness to the other nations that they are God's people. The

Hebrews celebrate Passover on the plain, offering and eating the feast in the form of unleavened cakes and parched grain and the produce of the land. The fall of manna ceases. They are no longer in the desert; now they are home. They have the food of the land with which to bless God in gratitude and remembrance. They eat the yield of the land of Canaan. Do we eat the yield of the Kingdom of God together in gratitude and remembrance?

The readings today feature food and taste—not just food for physical survival but food for the heart and soul, for dignity and hope, for a future freed from the past. Psalm 34 and its response, "Taste and see the goodness of the Lord," focus on an image of food. What do we offer in praise of God, in thanksgiving and blessing, in words that others can hear and take heart from? Are the lowly made glad because of our words and the way we put them into practice? We are meant to glorify God together and to extol God's name. We have sought out God, and God has delivered us. In turn, we are to save the afflicted from fear and distress as God has saved us. Now is a time for feasting, for rejoicing.

Paul's words to the Corinthians are heartening: "If anyone is in Christ, they are a new creation." Through the work of God in Christ we are a new people. We are reconciled to God through Christ, and we have been entrusted with the message of reconciliation and its ministry of forgiveness, justice, healing, restoration, atonement, of removing reproach from others, of wiping away shame, of bringing radiance to the faces of those who have been weighed down. We are ambassadors with Christ for others. God now appeals through us as once God appealed to us through Jesus. Paul implores, "In Christ's name: be reconciled to God!" It seems like a command. We are to be the very holiness of God and so attract all men and women home, back to God, through our persons, communities, works, words, and mercy.

Then there is the familiar story in Luke of the prodigal son, the lost son. It is a magical story, a parable. The introduction is crucial to our understanding of the story. Jesus is seated at table—an image of eucharist for Luke's community—with tax-collectors and sinners. They are listening, and the Pharisees and scribes are murmuring. Their complaint is that Jesus welcomes sinners and eats with them. So Jesus tells them all a story, one that is specifically directed at the religious leaders.

A man has two sons. The younger wants his inheritance immediately, and the father, going against all tradition (property was usually deeded by law to the eldest son, who took care of his siblings in his father's name), splits up his property and gives half to the younger son. The younger son sells his share of the land and squanders the proceeds. He leaves his father's house, his brother, his family, his nation, his religion, and his heritage. Eventually he is left alone, reduced to feeding pigs on a stranger's land and hesitant even to ask for the leftovers that the pigs won't eat.

He comes to his senses (is this true repentance or the cry of his stomach?) and starts plotting how he can go home with some dignity. He prepares a speech filled with false humility designed to get his father to take him back and even pay him to live and work in his own home. This is after he has lost half of his father's heritage and his brother's inheritance! The young man sounds rotten; there is no repentance here, just base self-interest. He's going home because he has no other choice. He's in need, hungry. So he sets off for home.

Now the story gets strange. The father sees him coming from afar. How? Houses were clustered together, surrounded by the market and business area and then fields and the roads. The father must have gone out every day to look for his son, hoping against hope that he would come home. The father knows that if he does, he'll need protection from relatives and neighbors angered by the sale of the family land. The son might be stoned, spit upon, cursed, reviled.

The father is not typical. He cares only for his child, even though he is grown and stupid, a public sinner, a loss to the community. So the father runs out to him, cuts off his prepared speech, calls his servants, and puts his own robe, sandals, and ring (which belong by right to the older son) on him. Then the father orders a feast, a big public celebration to which all will be invited.

Meanwhile the dutiful son, intent on inheriting what's left and keeping an eye on his inheritance, hears the commotion and asks a servant what is happening. (Note that in Luke the servant always represents Jesus.) The elder brother refuses to go in. So the father, humiliated again in the presence of all his neighbors and relatives, goes out again, this time to plead with his other son.

Now the elder son reveals his greed and insensitivity to his father's will and love and life. He cuts himself off from both his brother and his father. He describes himself not as a son but as a slave. He has no awareness whatsoever of his relationship with his father, his responsibilities to his brother. *He* should have been out looking for his younger brother in order to save his father from such pain and public humiliation. But he cares only for his own life and possessions and friends.

So now the story is laid out. The father is as blunt and to the point as God will be with us, especially those of us who refuse to acknowledge that we are sinners. We are all sinners, though some of us sin differently in "more acceptable" ways, ways ignored more easily by others, but obviously not by God. The father personally repeats to the stubborn and cold-hearted elder son: "We had to celebrate and rejoice! This brother of yours was dead and has come back to life. He was lost, and is found!" This implies that the elder brother is still dead and lost unless he welcomes his brother back. We all must rejoice over any and all sinners who return to God, for whatever reasons. After all, the older son is reminded by his father, "You are with me always, and everything I have is yours."

There is a saying among storytellers that the story begins when the storyteller stops talking. In this parable what happens next? Does the father go back alone, without the elder brother? This is what happens with the group to whom Jesus is telling the story, except for a few. How does the meeting in public between the two brothers go if the older does come in? What does the younger brother do in restitution, restoration, atonement? What does the elder brother do? The two brothers are now equals because the father has given the robe (baptismal garment), sandals (discipleship), and ring (seal of inheritance, gifts of the Spirit) to the younger brother. Do they live in harmony? And what of the servant who gave the news to the older brother? Jesus is killed because of the message he brings of the mercy and compassion of God and our need to rejoice over one another.

What of our community? Do we celebrate eucharist? Do we need forgiveness and mercy? Do we atone for what we have done and refused to do? With whom do we refuse to eat or celebrate as brother and sister? From whom do we separate ourselves? How do we hinder the coming of reconciliation and mercy to others in the world by our insensitivity, selfishness, sin, and ingratitude? Are we always with God and yet blind and unaware of what we should be doing in faith for others as their older brothers and sisters?

In Africa villages are spread out along roads and the churches are built in small open spaces. There is a tradition of pulling up grass on the way to church and offering it to anyone you have wronged, hurt, or are at odds with before you come into the building to worship. We need forgiveness and reconciliation, but we also need to offer them to others before asking God for ourselves. As we pray in the Lord's Prayer, "Forgive us our trespasses as we forgive those who trespass against us."

Often in these African communities, when they gather together to celebrate the Word, feuds, disagreements, and hatreds are brought up by the leaders. If all members of the community do not seek forgiveness and offer each other signs of peace, then the community does not celebrate the eucharist. The members cannot, for the body is at odds with itself.

How does the ritual of reconciliation look in our lives? Does it take on different forms with different people: spouse, children, friends, family, co-workers, students, members of the parish, strangers? We need to look carefully at how we seek forgiveness and open the door to a better way of relating. It can start with a phone call, a touch on the shoulder, a gift, a letter or card, flowers, a hug, a kiss, a handshake, a shared meal—somehow getting closer to the other. What did God do? He sent Jesus.

There are many stories on this theme. This one is from the oral tradition of Yemen. I read it once in a collection of Jewish stories for children in a bookstore in San Francisco. It's called "The Palace of Bird Beaks."

✙ Once upon a time there was a king named Solomon, who was known throughout the world for his wisdom. He could command the winds and the birds to come whenever he called them. He even knew the languages of all the birds and animals of the earth.

Now it so happened that one of King Solomon's wives was soon to have a birthday. The king asked her what gift she would like from him. She exclaimed, "I want something that no other queen on earth has ever had. Build me a palace made of bird beaks. There are so many of them." And out of love for his wife, Solomon answered, "It shall be done, my dear. A palace of bird beaks shall be yours."

Then King Solomon called forth all the birds in the world and ordered them to come to his palace prepared to give up their beaks. Before even a day had gone by, thousands upon thousands of birds filled the sky, beating their wings and swooping down to the palace. All of them came, the strong eagle, tiny hummingbirds, bright bluebirds, mockingbirds, doves and pigeons, ducks—every bird that lived on the face of the earth. The birds were distraught at having to give up their beaks. What a stupid idea this queen had. Did she have nothing else to do all day but think up such things? But what could they do? Soon every bird had flocked to the palace except one—the hoopoe—a little bird with colorful feathers and a fine pointed beak.

As time passed and the hoopoe did not arrive, the king became angry. "Fetch the hoopoe and bring it here to me!" he shouted to his servants. "Let it be punished for failing to obey the king!"

At last the hoopoe was brought before the king. "Where have you been?" King Solomon demanded. "Why have you kept me waiting?"

"Please, your majesty, do not be angry with me," said the hoopoe. "I have been flying to the ends of the earth. I have seen gardens, forests, oceans, deserts. From all that I have seen, I have gained much wisdom, so that I may serve you well. Punish me if you must, but first give me a chance to prove to you that I have not just been flying lazily about. Let me ask you three riddles. If there is one that you can't answer, then spare my life."

The other birds gasped. How shocked they were that a bird dared bargain with the king! But King Solomon admired this bold little creature, and he accepted the challenge. "Very well," he said, "ask your riddles. After all, how can your wisdom be compared to the wisdom of a king?"

So the hoopoe spoke. "This is the first riddle. Tell me, your majesty, who is it who was never born and has never died?"

The king did not even pause to think. "The Lord of the world, blessed be he," he said at once. And as he spoke, the king thought to himself, "The Lord of the world created all the creatures of the world to be free."

The hoopoe continued. "Here is the second riddle. Tell me, your majesty, what water never rises from the ground and never falls from the sky?"

King Solomon smiled for he knew that answer too. "The answer is a tear," he said, "a tear that falls from an eye that cries in sadness." As he finished answering, King Solomon looked around and saw all the birds stretched out before him, waiting sadly, helplessly, many with tears in their eyes, for their beaks to be cut off. The king was saddened too, and a tear came to his eyes.

Now a strange thing happened. Although King Solomon was certain that his wisdom was perfect, for just a moment it occurred to him that perhaps he had done a foolish and unwise thing in agreeing to build a palace of bird beaks.

Then the hoopoe spoke again. This time its voice trembled, for it had only one riddle left, only one more chance to save itself. "Your majesty, what is it that is delicate enough to put food in a baby's mouth, yet strong enough to bore holes in the hardest wood?"

It did not take King Solomon long to reply. "Why, a bird's beak of course!" he answered. And looking around at that great gathering of birds, he realized how special these creatures were, and how very precious their beaks were to them.

Meanwhile, the hoopoe bowed its head. "Punish me as you will, your majesty, for you have answered my three riddles." It waited in silence to hear the harsh punishment of the king.

But the king was smiling. "Dear hoopoe," he spoke in a loud voice so that all the birds could hear, "I am known throughout the world for my wisdom, yet you are the one who is truly wise. You have shown me that a king should never be too proud to admit that he has made a mistake. You have shown me that mercy is more important than wisdom. I have decided not to build a palace of bird beaks after all."

At this, all the birds wanted to flap their wings in joy and sing, but they did not dare to interrupt the king. "For your wisdom you shall be rewarded, not punished," said the king. He called forth the royal jeweler and bade him make the bird a small crown, much like the crown he himself wore. When the crown was finished, King Solomon placed it upon the head of the hoopoe.

So it is that to this day the hoopoe wears a crown on its forehead, to remind all the birds who see it of the reward of King Solomon and the wisdom of the bird who saved their beaks. And all the humans who see the crown as the hoopoe flies are reminded that mercy is better than wisdom.

We can rely on and even come to demand mercy from God, but if we accept God's mercy then we must in turn give that mercy unbounded to all we meet in our lives. Unmitigated mercy can only be responded to with open-handed forgiveness of others. The psalm tells us, "Look to God that you may be radiant with joy, and your faces may not blush with shame. For when the afflicted one called out, the Lord heard and from all their distress he saved them" (Psalm 34:5-6). We are saved.

The Sufi masters say that it is the nature of God to forgive. Once when a man approached the Prophet, he begged him to pray for him, specifically that he would never sin again. The Prophet refused, saying that if the man did not sin, he would not need the forgiveness of God and would begin to think he was better than others. God will always forgive. It is up to us to atone, to restore the balance, and to repair the breach in relationships and in the world where our sin has torn holes.

The story of the lost son is neither easy nor pleasant. It reveals the hardness of our hearts. It calls us to atone, restore, and repair. We are designated ambassadors of Christ, expected to go to great lengths, any lengths really, to bring others back home.

The parable is clear. The relationship of the sons to the father is the vertical dimension of the cross, and the relationship of the brothers to each other is the horizontal dimension. A gap in either one reveals us as either murmuring hypocrites or those who take God's mercy for granted and are without gratitude. Each one of us needs forgiveness, more than we know or wish to acknowledge.

I once had students write a letter to the father in this parable, pretending they were his wife. I also had them write a letter to each of the sons from their mother. What role did she play as ambassador to her children, as support to her husband? What pain and sorrow did she bear as she watched her children destroying each other and insulting their father. Although she is not mentioned in the story, the technique of midrash, of reading under and through an account to come up with another perspective, can lead us to new insight.

My grandmother—my nana—used to tell me that when we get to heaven we're probably going to be very surprised at who got us there, who prayed us home, who forgave us, and who stood in the breach on our behalf. She said it with that look that meant a second part of the lesson was yet to come. The second part was whom *I* was going to get into heaven. Was I spending my time praying for people? restoring and repairing breaches? and doing penance for others in the world?

Isaiah 58 reminds us that God will always guide us and give us relief in desert places if we do away with the yoke, the clenched fist, the wicked word, and give of our bread to the hungry and relief to the oppressed. That is not a far cry from forgiveness, sitting down to table and sharing the eucharist with those we have wronged and those who have sinned against us. If we do these things we will be "like a watered garden, like a spring of water whose waters never run dry." We will rebuild ancient ruins and build up old foundations and we will be called "breach-mender" and "restorer of ruined houses.' That is not a bad way to be remembered.

Sunday of the Fifth Week of Lent

Isaiah 43:16-21
Philippians 3:8-14
John 8:1-11

We are not to give any thought to what's behind us, only to what lies ahead. Like Paul, our entire attention must be on the finish line of the race. We must look for the power flowing from the resurrection and share in Jesus' sufferings. Even in the gospel, when the woman is caught in sin, Jesus says: "You may go. But from now on, avoid this sin." There is no condemnation.

There is no condemnation from God today for what we have done or failed to do, only an exhortation to go our way, the way of the cross, and turn toward resurrection and new life. It is time to be formed in the pattern of Jesus' death, so that we may arrive at life. Now the tension mounts, the pain grows, the hate against Jesus and his message is palpable. His enemies are intent on tripping him up, catching him in his own words, so that they will have something to use against him. The forces of evil are arrayed against the forces of mercy. But we are assured, in the words of Teresa of Avila, that "the mules are packed, they are kicking, the road will be rocky, but the destination is sure."

Again we look at the ancient stories of salvation, the run to freedom and the destruction of the oppressors in Egypt. This is the way of Jesus, the way of discipleship, the way of the cross, the way of the Kingdom of God. And the waters of the desert and wasteland spring up for us to drink. God has formed and chosen us so that we might sing God's praise. We, the people of God, live to announce the goodness of God and God's works of reconciliation, mercy, and justice. This is another creation account. God is doing new things.

We sing our response to Psalm 126: "The Lord has done great things for us; we are filled with joy." This is the wonder and sheer delight expressed when the captives of Zion could finally return. They were ecstatic, filled with laughter, delirious with joy. Even the other nations see and acknowledge the great things that God does for them and their gladness in God. The psalm ends with a prayer to "restore our fortunes, O Lord, like the torrents in the southern desert"; the torrents there are fast, furious, unexpected, drenching. All the images are those of surfeit, excess, overflow. But there is also the reminder that the seed must be sown in tears, though in the end there will be rejoicing.

Paul's words to the Philippians are remarkable. He has come to rate all as loss in light of knowledge of Jesus Christ. Paul has forfeited everything, given up everything. His only wealth is Christ, the Word, mercy, forgiveness, healing, thanksgiving, so that he may be in Christ, with no justice of his own, only God's hunger for justice, holiness, and compassion. This comes through faith in Christ Jesus, clinging to God in Christ, living in Christ. Paul announces: "I wish to know Christ and the power flowing from his resurrection; likewise to know how to share in his sufferings by being formed into the pattern of his death."

Death is begun in baptism and is lived out in commitment and obedience, especially in community. Paul hasn't reached his goal yet, but he is racing to grasp the prize, which is fullness of spirit in Christ. There is no thought of what is behind, only of what lies ahead: crucifixion, death, resurrection, and the coming of the Spirit to transform all the earth and its people. Paul runs toward life in Christ Jesus. With only two weeks until Passover, the paschal mystery of our own life, death, and resurrection as a people of God, are we too intent for this one thing alone? Do we seek only the power flowing from the resurrection? We must pray for this kind of faith and hope and passionate devotion to God.

What is it like to run a race? Runners don't look back, because it breaks their stride and concentration. They keep thinking ahead to the finish line and how they have to run now. They pass on the baton, reaching out to another. It is the responsibility of the next runner to take the baton as well as to pass it on as the last act of the race.

The Greeks raced naked, so that nothing would get in the way of their finishing the race. We are called to be stripped of everything but the cross so that we can run freely. We are clothed only in a white garment of hope and resurrection, the new creation that Jesus has passed onto us in his cross and glory. We are called today to stand and pray for the strength to strip ourselves of everything that makes running difficult.

The gospel reading jumps to the gospel of John for the story of a woman caught in adultery and publicly forgiven by Jesus. The story shows us how to celebrate forgiveness, reconciliation, and penance in the community. Sin and forgiveness are never just private or personal affairs.

The backdrop of the story is the Mount of Olives, where Jesus went out to pray throughout the night. (Jesus always prays before confrontations.) At daybreak he reappears in the Temple area and the people start coming to him. The emphasis is on "to him." He himself is now the Temple, and he sits down and teaches them. The scribes and Pharisees bring forward a woman who had been caught in adultery. We should note that only one person is led forward, but that it takes two to commit adultery. Her partner is conspicuously absent from this encounter. Perhaps she was set up to get at Jesus. She is useful for what they have in mind: trapping Jesus publicly. They make her stand there in front of everyone. She is not a person but a thing, bait to set the trap. They pose the question: "Teacher, this woman has been caught in the act of adultery. In the law, Moses ordered such women to be stoned. What do you have to say about the case?"

The scribes and Pharisees think that however Jesus responds they can accuse him. If he sides with the woman and forgives her, as he is often wont to do in public, he will make friends with the people but he will publicly break the Law of Moses—just what they want him to do. If he upholds their interpretation of the Law of Moses, the people will turn from him.

But Jesus, especially in John's gospel, refuses to be drawn into such traps or to play by their rules. He refuses to look at the Law the way they do. He refuses to act in the way they expect. He refuses to validate their position or their God. He is about his Father's will and the underlying law of compassion and mercy; he is not about the letter and harshness of a law used to serve destructive ends. Jesus bends down and starts tracing on the ground with his finger. They persist in their questioning. He is still silent. He refuses to condemn her. He does nothing but write on the ground.

Perhaps he is livid with rage, sad, tender of her, angry at their hypocrisy. He gives them time to see their own hate and selfishness and untruth, but they refuse. So he speaks to them: "Let the one among you who has no sin be the first to cast a stone at her." Blunt and to the point. They have singled her and her sin out as worthy of the death penalty, in which all participate in the execution righteously according to the law. They have no regard for her as a person or for their own sin in setting her up, or for setting Jesus up.

Jesus reminds them of what they have forgotten: we are all sinners, all worthy of death and punishment. It is God alone who condemns, the God of the living and the dead. This reading is often used to teach that Jesus opposed the death penalty for sin, especially for sexual offenses. But more to the point, Jesus knows that soon he himself will be in her predicament. He will be lied against and condemned to death, handed over to the Romans for a legal execution. All this will be according to the law.

One by one the elders drift away. All those he was teaching, the bystanders, and the curious have disappeared. A second time he bends down and writes on the ground. Some people like to think he was writing down the sins of the scribes and Pharisees. Whatever he is writing, Jesus is bent over, kneeling at the woman's feet. Finally Jesus straightens up (having borne the burden of sin that will bend him over on the way of the cross) and speaks to her (using the formal title of honor and respect he uses with his mother, both at Cana and at the foot of the cross): "Woman, where did they all disappear to? Has no one condemned you?" She answers him: "No sir, no one." And Jesus is kind: "Nor do I condemn you. You may go. But from now on, avoid this sin."

She is set free, but gently reminded to avoid sin. Jesus acknowledges her part in the sin, but to her alone, after reminding all (including us) of our universal reality of being sinners. We have no right to condemn another, let alone exact punishment or become another's executioner. Jesus will bear the brunt and the burden of all sin. Jesus accepts the truth of who we are and are not. He humbles himself before us always, so that we can see ourselves and humble ourselves before God.

This is the last Sunday of Lent. Next come the passion accounts, the procession of palms, the way of the cross. We stand before Jesus as sinners in need of confession, repentance, and change. We are all condemned under the law, at the whim of those in power; we are all offered forgiveness in the cross of Christ, called to be ambassadors of reconciliation.

The actions of the scribes and Pharisees seem inhuman and cruel, but we are not far removed from them. Although the American bishops and John Paul II's encyclical letter on the culture of death call for abolishing the death penalty, alarming numbers of Catholics and Christians support it for certain crimes. Similarly, the recent trend toward vindictive punishment reveals an intent to blame and exact pain and death without any recourse to our own faith traditions. We all harbor violence and hatred in our hearts. We make others into enemies and refuse to forgive them, to speak with them, to eat with them. We refuse to allow those we claim have wronged us or our loved ones or our nation to have any sort of life with us.

John's gospel is layered with symbols. Many of the stories, such as this one, appear only in John. Oftentimes the individuals—the woman at the well, the man born blind, the man at the pool, the woman caught in adultery—stand for someone else, for groups such as catechumens, disciples, those who refuse to believe even after having met Jesus.

The woman caught in adultery represents Israel, whose people are both the chosen of Yahweh and unfaithful, caught in terrible acts of impurity, dishonesty, and unfaithfulness to the God of the covenant.

This woman also represents us: our church, our community, our parish. We are caught. We will not be condemned, but we will be told to avoid unfaithfulness and promiscuous behavior, unaware of how our sin can be used to destroy those who are good and holy. Our example and our behavior can give scandal, and our sin can bend others who are already under the weight of sin and discouragement. Although God does not condemn us, we must be careful and diligent not to condemn others politically, socially, economically, religiously. We must be careful not to bait others or to try to catch them in their sin or count their transgressions against them. One thing we all intimately share as humans is sin. It is unique to each of us and, sadly, rather mundane and alike in its mangling of others' lives and our own.

There is a Jewish tale told in eastern Europe that puts us in our place, reminding us of things we tend to forget quickly.

✛ Once upon a time there were three students who wanted to study with a famous rabbi. They followed him from a distance, listening and working hard, trying to save their money so that they could travel to where he dwelled and join his group of students. They were good friends and did everything together.

Finally, one of them had an idea. "Let's go off and find the man even if we don't have enough money or food for the journey. As we stop in the villages along the way, we'll tell the people we're rabbis and that we are on our way to meet with our great teacher. They will help us and be generous to us; you know how hospitable our people are."

The others were uneasy with the idea, but they really did want to study with the rabbi. They promised each other solemnly that when they returned they would share their knowledge with all who had aided them.

They set off, and everything went incredibly well. In each village they were welcomed, fed and cared for, often in the houses of the wealthiest, and then sent on their way the next day with food for the journey. They traveled for weeks in this manner and were easing into their new roles as rabbis and teachers, men of prayer and holiness.

One day they came to a town and asked for food and shelter, as was their custom, sharing their story in the marketplace so that word would get around. They were offered lodging for the night. They settled down and were saying their prayers when there was a knock at the door. A frantic man, the mayor of the town, was at the door. His daughter was terribly sick, dying. Would one of the rabbis, one of the holy ones, come and pray over her, lay a hand on her, and beg the Holy One, blessed be his Name, to have mercy on her parents and let her live?

The students were struck to the heart, terrified. What were they to do? They couldn't just say who they really were—nobodies who had been lying all along. One of them moved quickly, eyeing his friends sharply. He went with the man, telling him that he would, of course, pray to God for the health and well-being of the girl.

He was gone a long time and came back exhausted and fearful. They caught a few hours sleep and left before dawn. He was sure that the child would die before the sun came up, and he wanted to be far away from the village. He was not a rabbi, just a student impersonating a holy man. A true holy man would be able to bend the arm and heart of God and bring the man's daughter back to him.

They traveled on, sobered by the experience, and they finally caught up with the real rabbi. They stayed with him for many months, listening and learning, amazed at his wisdom and knowledge. Finally, as they went to take their leave, the rabbi looked at them, especially at the young man who had prayed over the young girl. He spoke earnestly to them. "You must return to all the villages and tell the people of your deception and dishonesty. Now you are teachers in your own right and you must be truthful." They swallowed hard, but they knew that he was right. In village after village they apologized for

their lies, and to their surprise, they were easily forgiven
and welcomed once again, fed, and cared for as teachers.

But then they drew near to the town where the young
girl had lain dying. They were all afraid, especially the
young man who had gone to pray over the child. They
steeled themselves and entered the village. Immediately
there was a commotion, a stirring all around them. The
villagers pointed at them and whispered behind their
backs. This was going to be difficult. Obviously the girl
had died, and the mayor would not take kindly to their
returning, let alone their acknowledgment that they had
lied to him and the others.

Just then the mayor appeared. He ran to them, wav-
ing his arms wildly. He grabbed the young man in his
arms, covering him with tears and kisses and blessings.
The girl lived. Within the day she had recovered. Truly
the goodness of the Holy One was to be blessed. They
all tried to explain, but the man would have none of it.
They would stay in his house that night and as long as
they wanted to stay. Such men were welcome in this village.

That night, after all the festivities had died down, the
young man looked up from his prayers to see his two
friends looking at him oddly. "What is it?" he queried them.

They muttered about prayer and power and then asked
him outright, "Are you a holy one? Have you kept it from
us all along? After all, you did bring that child back from
the brink of death. You yourself said that she wouldn't
make it through the night."

The young man was struck dumb. Then, shaking his
head, he asked forgiveness. "Brothers, remember, we all
lied, we all deceived. But God's mercy and goodness
were stronger than our sin. In the presence of God we
are all pretenders, but the Holy One will not allow that to
cripple his own holiness."

A stunning line: in the presence of God, we are all pretenders. We all live lives of dishonesty, of deception. We must
remember that goodness comes through us, but only because God's mercy is stronger than our sin.

Rabbi Abraham Joshua Heschel had a saying: "It takes three things to attain a sense of significant being: God, a soul, and a moment. And the three are always here. Just to be is a blessing. Just to live is holy." This is especially so in the story from today's gospel. There is God. There is the soul of the woman caught in sin, the people of Israel caught in unfaithfulness. There is the church and all of us caught in our sin. And there is the moment. It is given as a blessing. We can be holy because of God. We must remember.

A Jewish story from the Talmud tells of an aged man who was invited to Abraham's tent in hospitality but who refused to join Abraham in prayer to the one God. Abraham drove him out when he learned that he was a fire-worshiper. Later that night God appeared to Abraham in a dream and said, "I have borne with that ignorant man for over seventy years. Could you not have been patient with him for one night?" God is infinitely patient with us and our sin, our weaknesses and our foibles. The least we can do is be patient with one another, and then, as Jesus does, tell one another to avoid this or that sin.

Let us pray for one another in words from the Third Scrutiny:

Father of eternal life, you are a God, not of the dead, but of the living. You sent your Son to proclaim the good news of life, to rescue us from the kingdom of death and to pass onto us the power of the resurrection. Bless this people and free us from the power of evil. May we receive new life from Christ who urges us "to go our way and sin no more" and may we bear witness to you in your cross and suffering and so, know the power of your resurrection. We ask this through Christ our Lord. Amen.

Do you promise to strip yourself of anything that keeps you from running your race to the finish?

Response: We do.

Do you promise to lay aside anything that causes others to stumble on their race to the finish? (*We do.*)

Do you promise to be patient with the weaknesses of others as God is patient with your sin? (*We do.*)

Do you promise to forgive, to not condemn others, but to exhort them to avoid sin? (*We do.*)

Do you promise to be careful of people, careful of the truth and careful of God's mercy in your own life, holding it with gratitude and sharing it freely with others? (*We do.*)

Do you promise to remember that we are all pretenders and in need of the mercy of God? (*We do.*)

May God who has chosen us to run this race and to serve him so that we might be united to Christ in his death and resurrection be strengthened by his grace and spirit and freed from sin. May we conquer all bitterness and sadness and help one another to finish the race. May we rely on all those who have shed their blood in the defense and honor of their faith and life, and take courage from Christ who gave his life so that we might be free. We ask this in the name of Jesus who is Lord for ever and ever. Amen.

Passion/Palm Sunday

From the Procession with Palms, Luke 19:28-40
Isaiah 50:4-7
Philippians 2:6-11
The Passion Account, Luke 22:14-23, 56

We begin with our procession, and Jesus goes ahead with his ascent to Jerusalem. He climbs to the mountain of the Lord, the place of glory and execution, the place where the prophets are murdered and truth confronts power. As he approaches Bethany and Bethphage, outside of Jerusalem, and the Mount of Olives, he sends two of his disciples with instructions to prepare the Passover ritual. He is specific about his entrance into Jerusalem at the time of the feast. They are to find an ass that has not yet been ridden and untie it and bring it to him. It happens exactly as he says. When they return with the ass, they lay their cloaks on it and help him to mount. He descends from the Mount of Olives and the people, along with his disciples, begin to rejoice and praise God loudly for the display of power they have seen. They are caught up in the moment. There are no palm branches in Luke, only cloaks, the most treasured and expensive of garments, and the song that is sung is the echo of the song of the angels on the night of Jesus' birth into the world: "Peace in heaven and glory in the highest!"

The Pharisees are annoyed. "Teacher," they say, "rebuke your disciples." And Jesus responds: if they were to keep silence, the very stones would cry out. Stones remind us of the temptations, the falling towers, stones taken up to kill.

Jesus allows the disciples to rejoice and sing and praise God. This is another step on the road to the cross, the beginning of glory. The week will contain all of suffering, life and death, passion and betrayal, hope and despair, crucifixion and resurrection—all for the glory of God and peace on earth and in heaven.

With this reading Passion Week begins. In Luke's account Jesus is the Suffering Servant of God who relies on God alone. He is not disgraced, no matter what the world thinks or how the world judges. Jesus accepts death, even death on a cross, and prays to God to save him, trusting in God's power. We are reminded that we are the followers of Jesus, those who have stood by him in his temptations. We are to listen to the Passion account as Jesus' friends—those who stand by him at a distance, or who leave him. Luke's account reminds us that the religious authorities did not know what to do with Jesus and conspired with the government to get rid of him. Even though the two groups were bitter enemies, they plotted together to kill Jesus. Pilate passes him to Herod, then Herod passes him back to Pilate. Pilate passes the blame to the people. It is time for us to stand and take responsibility for what we pass on to others and to stand with Jesus in his passion and death, so that we can stand with him in resurrection and glory.

Holy Week is a traditional time in many places, a time of special foods: hot cross buns, light fare, shared bread. In others it means observance of silence on Friday, pilgrimages, more prayer, fasting, the *Desciendemento* (the taking down of Jesus from the cross on Good Friday night). The palms we receive are a victory symbol. At the beginning of the week and at the end we will mix fervent songs of Hosanna and deep silence, praising Jesus for his love and praying silently as he dies. It is a time to stand by Jesus. It is a time to put our life on the line with Jesus, to be obedient unto death, even death on a cross. It is time to say a word to rouse others in hope and courage. It is time to go to the cross and be buried with Jesus.

Traditionally people weave their pieces of palm into crosses. We reverence this symbol of liberation and salvation. We kiss it, sign ourselves with it, bow and kneel before it. The cross stands for everything that Jesus was willing to take up on our behalf. It is a symbol of the love of God the Father for us in Jesus, through the power of the Spirit. It is a sign of strength and of protection against evil and fear. It is a sign of our salvation and life in God. The cross is also a sign of the power of nonviolent resistance, of love and truth and mercy, which are always stronger than hate and lies and violence.

The readings that begin the Palm Sunday liturgy are always the same—the description of the Suffering Servant, the model for all believers and disciples who are called to speak a word to the weary. The word will rouse them to courage and endurance and give them ears to hear, and a heart and body that do not rebel in the face of suffering, persecution, torture, and inhumanity. But the readings also describe believers who trust that they will not be disgraced before God. So we set our faces like flint, knowing that we will not be put to shame. Our trust, hope, and strength are in God alone. There are only two places to stand—with the victims or with those who oppress them.

Psalm 22 with its refrain, "My God, my God, why have you abandoned me?," is a cry of pain, of anguish, of hope, of one in terrible torment at the hands of others. It is a desperate cry to God, who hears the cry of the poor. The psalm describes the victim of injustice and hate—scorned, mocked, insulted, brutalized in body and soul—and it describes the descent into hell of those who do such evil to other human beings. But it ends with a plea: "O Lord, be not far from me; O my help, hasten to aid me." God is near to those who suffer and to the prophets who stand up for the poor of the earth. God is near to them in their need.

Paul's letter to the Philippians is the exhortation to those preparing for baptism and for a public commitment to following Jesus. It encourages them to deny themselves, to pick up their crosses and go after Jesus, who is now close to glory. It is the proclamation of the Philippian community, its declaration of faith that Jesus, the servant, humble to death on a cross, accepted fully what it meant to be human among us. Because of the incarnation and Jesus' great love, God will exalt and raise him up along with all who believe in him and stand with him in death. We are called to worship, to bend with Jesus, to pray in his name with all the world that Jesus Christ is Lord to the glory of God the Father. This week is about surrender, worship, obedience, and faithfulness with Jesus, giving ourselves to God with Jesus and being accepted as the children of God, who live, die, and rise in the Spirit and live "no longer for ourselves alone, but hidden with Christ in God."

The Passion account according to Luke begins with the Passover meal, the eucharist. The context of the meal is suffering, loss, and betrayal—and friendship, both friendship that is lacking and friendship that is love unto death, the friendship of Jesus. The telling of the story of the eucharist leads directly into the betrayal by those in the community: the one who sets him up, and those who will run away in their fear. Jesus is the Suffering Servant, aligned with those who are betrayed and lost to the earth and their loved ones. But even in the midst of the Passover ritual a dispute arises about who among his followers is the greatest. Luke's gospel is about power. Jesus explains clearly that the greatest in his Kingdom is the one who is the lowest. In Jesus' Kingdom, service gives power.

Jesus reminds Simon that he will betray him before the cock crows three times. Peter still does not know or take responsibility for his own sins and weaknesses or understand how they affect the community.

The meal is one of tenderness and great sadness. There is a further discussion, revealing again that the disciples do not understand allusions to swords, violence, and the coming persecution. They have not learned that, for Jesus, the sword is the word of God. Jesus ends the meal with "Enough," and they leave for the garden at the Mount of Olives.

Jesus prays there and invites his friends to pray with him. The disciples eventually sleep. Jesus falls before his Father and bends to the Father's will, to the reality of being human and subject to death and to the power and hate of the world. He prays for courage, acceptance, and endurance, and he reminds those who sleep—and who are still unaware of the struggle for good and evil—to pray that they will not be subjected to the trial or succumb to it.

Jesus is betrayed by Judas with an embrace and a kiss. Again there are swords. Again "Enough!" he says. Still, he heals those hurt by violence. For the moment evil triumphs, and Jesus is arrested and led away. Jesus is taken inside the high priest's house, and he is lied about in testimony there. Then he is lied about outside, by Peter in response to the serving woman's questioning of his following of Jesus. The rooster crows, and Peter weeps bitterly.

Evil and hatred rise against Jesus, and he is tortured and insulted. In the morning he is brought before Pilate. Pilate sends him to Herod, and Herod insults him further. Jesus will not even speak to Herod. Then he is returned to Pilate. There is collusion here between church and state. They agree that this man is a problem, dangerous.

Pilate takes on the people and the priests. He frees Barabbas and gives Jesus to the crowd. Jesus is led away, carrying his cross, and Simon the Cyrenian, a black field worker, is recruited to help him carry his cross. Simon is forced into discipleship behind Jesus, but obviously stays, because we know his name and the names of his children. Jesus speaks along the way to some women of Jerusalem and redirects their pity to those who will follow him, to all those who suffer.

Jesus is crucified between two thieves, his garments divided among the soldiers. He forgives us all in the midst of his terrible agony. He is mocked by soldiers, onlookers, the people, the leaders, everyone. He is described publicly as the King of the Jews, although his Kingdom is one of mercy, forgiveness, peace, and nonviolent resistance to injustice. One thief curses him, but the second thief repents and finds his way into the Kingdom that very day. The curtain of the sanctuary is torn in two. At the end, Jesus gives his spirit into the hands of the Father and dies.

It is the centurion who makes a pronouncement of faith: "Surely this was an innocent man." Jesus' friends and the women of Galilee, named earlier in the gospel, stand at a distance and watch. Joseph of Arimathea takes the body and buries Jesus in his own tomb. The preparation day for the Passover feast begins as Jesus is put in the tomb. The people observe the sabbath. They obey the Law. Death reigns. This is the transition between the old and the new covenants, a radical disruption of all life and death. It is what we are called to attend to this week. It is up to us to decide where we stand.

This is Holy Week. It is time stripped down to the basics. How do we live? How do we die? Are we to perish by the sword or are we healers? Have we learned obedience by suffering? Do we believe that God can redeem even innocent and unjust suffering and death?

There is hope. Violence can stop. In the words of Simone Weil, "Pain and suffering are a kind of false currency passed from hand to hand until they reach someone who receives them but does not pass them on."

There is an ancient Russian legend that puts it clearly:

✢ Once upon a time two thieves repented. They had been partners in thieving and in injustice, and they now sought to make restitution and do penance together. They were both given the same penance by the monk. Each was to carry a cross across the desert and arrive at the city to celebrate his conversion.

Both started out enthusiastically, shouldering their fifty-pound crosses. The first day they struggled, sweating. The second and third days were torture; their water supply was getting low, the desert hotter, and their crosses seemed heavier. The desert stretched endlessly, its horizon blurry, but they plodded on.

Late on the third day, while they rested, one decided to shorten his cross. It was still his cross, just substantially shorter. The other decided to thin his out, and he cut it lengthwise. It was still his cross but much thinner. Both were more manageable, and the next two or three days went much easier. But the men were almost out of water. Finally, they came to water, but it was a rather wide canal that stretched for miles. They had been warned that this canal was filled with flesh-eating fish. They looked at their crosses. They could use them as bridges! The first laid his across the canal, but it was too short. He died in the desert. The other's cross was long enough, but when he put his weight on it, it broke and he fell into the water.

The holy man who tells this story eyes his listeners and asks them: "And your cross? Are you changing it, shortening it, thinning it, making your life easier? What will happen when you need your cross to bridge the gulf, to save you from evil and harm?" This week is for answering the hard questions.

Viktor Frankl, a Jewish psychiatrist interned in Auschwitz by the Nazis, wrote:

> We who lived in concentration camps can remember the men who walked through the huts comforting others, giving away their last piece of bread. They may have been few in number, but they offer sufficient proof that everything can be taken from a man but one thing: the last of the human freedoms—to choose one's attitude in any given set of circumstances—to choose one's own way.

This is surely true of Jesus, who in the midst of his pain chose to hand over his spirit to his Father, to forgive those who killed him, to offer paradise to a thief, and to pray. Jesus was and is always righteous, a holy man who shows us how to live in all circumstances and afflictions. He is the Son of Man, the Suffering Servant, the Holy One of God. He resists. He refuses to become like those who maltreat him and shame him and seek to break him. He refuses to die on their terms, just as he refused to live, to judge, to preach, and to love on their terms.

We are Christians. This week is prime learning for us. In the words of Teresa of Avila, "We always find that those who walked closest to Christ our Lord were those who had to bear the greatest trials."

There is a parable attributed to the Buddha that says he met a beggar on the road and said to him: "Having crossed the ocean of suffering, I must help others to cross it. Freed myself, I must set others free. This is the vow which I made in the past when I saw all that live in distress." Commenting on this parable in a speech given in Japan, Dom Paulo Cardinal Arns, the archbishop of Sao Paulo, Brazil, said:

> I rejoice to hear the words of Buddha and to see how often they are close to the Scriptures of my religion that are the basis of my life, my calling, my very being. In Japan and in Brazil we have crossed the ocean of suffering; we, all together, must help others to cross it. If we, through faith, have come to freedom, we must help others to be free. Buddha made this vow 2600 years ago. If we live by it, Buddhists and Christians, the world will know peace and we will have fulfilled our destiny. (*The Catholic Worker*, August-September 1994).

This week we walk with God toward the ocean of suffering and toward freedom, but we walk with faith and hope, and we walk together as a community. There is much we are reminded of, encouraged by, and much that will betray us. But God will stay faithful. Jesus stays faithful. We try to learn and understand and accept. Here is a story, a tale of the Sufi, to help us walk.

✢ A holy man was on his way to Mecca (the holy city of Islam). He had walked all night and was weary. Finally, he decided to sleep for a few hours before the light and then go into the city to pray when he was more alert and rested. He lay down on the ground and fell sound asleep. However, just as the light was coming, another man traveling to Mecca stumbled over him in the shadows. He didn't wake him, since he was sleeping so heavily. Then the man bent over him and shook him rudely awake. He had recognized him as a preacher and a holy man by his dress, and he was shocked. Slowly the sleeping man woke and began to recognize his surroundings and remember where he was.

Eventually he heard the man berating him and accusing him: "What kind of preacher and holy man are you? You should know the law. You are always to pray and sleep and do what you can with your feet pointing toward God, toward the Holy City and here you are sprawled out pointing to nothing."

Slowly the preacher sat up and looked at the man in front of him. "Sir," he said, "you say that I am to sleep with my feet pointing toward God. Is there any place I could sleep or any direction I could face where I wouldn't be pointing toward God?" And he turned over and went back to sleep for a few more moments.

It is Holy Week, the last week of Lent, the last week of turning our lives around so that no matter what we do, we are pointing toward God. And God *is* everywhere, especially in places where we do not always think to look. Holy Week points out that God is found, especially in places of suffering, death, betrayal, injustice, mockery, loneliness, and isolation. God is present in places where we need to trust God, continue to pray, and point out to all who watch us that all that we do and all that we are point to God. This is the way Jesus pointed to God, with humility, as a slave and a servant, with obedience, truth, compassion, and faith, accepting all from the hand of God but living fully human.

It is time to rouse each other with a word that speaks to the weary among us. It is time to send one another out to point to God in a world that does not see God hidden among us in those who are mocked and victimized. If we do not seek God, we will miss the glory of their faces made radant in the Easter light that awaits us, awakes us at this week's end.

We go in peace, to love and serve the Lord and one another. Let us sign ourselves with the cross in memory of incarnation and love come among us. In the name of the Father, in the name of the Son, and in the name of the Holy Spirit. Amen.

THE TRIDUUM

The Risen Lord

Holy Thursday

Mass of the Lord's Supper

Exodus 12:1-8, 11-14
1 Corinthians 11:23-26
John 13:1-15

Today is often called the feast of friends, the friends of God. But it is also a night of "re-membering," of putting back together the body of Christ, the church, the community of those who gather around the story (the word) and the bread (the flesh and blood) and become what they eat. The Jews begin Passover with the story. The youngest asks the question: Why is this night different from all others?

The ritual of Passover tells the story of terror and death, when the Angel of God passed over the doorways marked with the blood of the sacrificed lamb, and also about the wonder and marvelous works that God did for the chosen people in leading them out of Egypt, away from slavery and repression, through the desert of Sinai, and into the promised land. The ritual ends with the passionate cry: "Next year in Jerusalem!" a blessing and fervent prayer for the fullness of the promises set in motion so long ago.

Remembering is the essence of the ritual. It makes present in history the story and the promises. What God did in ages past for the chosen ones, God will do now for those gathered at table. The story continues in every generation. God waits for us to come.

This is the ritual that the Holy Thursday Mass is based upon, and yet there is more, for Jesus made significant changes in the ritual on the night before he died. We celebrate this night in the shadow of betrayal. It is a bittersweet night of intimacy, gifts given, and love expressed

The first reading begins with the account of the rite that is to be celebrated as a memorial in the first month of the Jewish calendar. It details the ritual slaying of the lamb, which is to be shared by a family alone or with other households so that the entire lamb is consumed. The lamb is slaughtered during the evening twilight, with the whole assembly of Israel as witness. Those who are to eat together take some of the blood of the lamb and mark their doorposts and the lintel of every house. How they are to eat the meal is specified: the foods are the lamb roasted, unleavened bread, and bitter herbs to remind them of preparation in haste and the bitter, long years of slavery and oppression when they could not worship their God. They eat the meal standing, with their belts and bags around their waists, sandals on their feet, and staff in hand, "like those who are in flight." Because they are. They are in flight from death, from slavery.

This is the Passover of the Lord, because on this night God will go through Egypt and strike down the firstborn, human and beast alike, executing judgment on all the gods of Egypt. This is a night of listening, believing, and clinging to others in fear and hope. It is a night of death that is the prelude to the beginning of life for a whole people. "Seeing the blood, I will pass over you; and no destructive blow will come upon you." The sight of the blood, seeping deep into the wood of the lintels of the doorways, is the mark and sign of salvation. And salvation is about bread, justice, and hope. This day is a memorial feast, a perpetual institution that all generations are commanded to remember, to celebrate the coming of the power of God into the world with freedom and lasting justice for those who cry out for help.

The images of unleavened bread, the lamb of God, and the blood marking those saved are woven through the Christian ritual as well, and yet they are more personal because the bread, the lamb, and the blood are the person and body of Jesus and what we become: the body of Christ in the world, a source of freedom and hope in the midst of terror and death for all who cry out to God.

We remember the dying and the rising of Jesus and on this night, his last meal with his friends, and his gift to them: his own flesh and blood. This memory is steeped in forgiveness, reconciliation, and atonement for the sins of the past, and rebirth. This night is a meal among friends, the sacrifice of the Lamb on the cross, and the resurrection—all braided into one reality. Johannes Metz calls this story the dangerous memory of the passion of Christ. It is dangerous and subversive, because what is seen as judgment and death by some is believed to be salvation and life by others. We must remember this night that the words "body of Christ" describe the eucharist and us, the people of God; we are to become bread for the world with the bread that we share this night.

It is not just the bread that is this rich source of strength and sustenance, it is also the blood. The psalm response sings: "Our blessing-cup is a communion with the blood of Christ" (Psalm 116). This reminds us what we are to do with our lives so that the ritual gestures of our worship are truly expressive of our self-giving. We are to make a return to the Lord for all the good that God has done for us. We are to take up the cup of salvation and call upon the name of the Lord—and we are to drink the cup of wine, blood, suffering, and salvation.

There is an immediate connection between eucharist and death: "Precious in the eyes of the Lord is the death of his faithful ones." All of our deaths are one in the dying of Jesus. All of us are servants, sons and daughters whose bonds have been loosed by our God, and so we offer a sacrifice of thanksgiving, vowing our lives to the Lord in the presence of one another. Our blessing-cup taken and shared proclaims that we trust in the blood that heals and reconciles the aches and wounds of the world caused by sin, evil, injustice, and violent hatred. The blood of Christ is poured into our wounds and we heal, scarred over and mindful of the suffering, but able to understand the pain of those who suffer unjustly and to share in their struggle to be free and whole. St. Paul reminds us: "I have been crucified with Christ. . . . I carry the marks of Jesus branded on my body" (Galatians 2:19; 6:17). In this ritual of eating and drinking with Jesus, we are in Christ, not just repeating his sacrifice and modeling our lives on his, but living in the wounds and heart and very body of Christ, together.

In the short, dense reading from Paul's letter to the Corinthians we are told to remember and to pass on what we have received from the Lord, exactly as we have been given it. The words, actions, and intent are all important. The setting is the night of betrayal. The movement of worship and thanksgiving to God is the offering. The priest takes bread, gives thanks, breaks it apart, and says: "This is my body, which is for you. Do this in remembrance of me." The cup is offered with the words: "This cup is the new covenant in my blood. Do this, whenever you drink it, in remembrance of me."

This is the core of our worship, lives, communities, and sacrifices, the core of our meaning as Christians. In eating the bread and drinking the cup we proclaim the death of the Lord until he comes! In remembering we are saved, the world is saved, the truth is told, the power of death is undone, and love is set loose in the midst of betrayal. There is really no way to explain this short passage; it is learned in living and understood in self-sacrifice, serving others, and remembering all that was taught to us by the words and works of Jesus.

The gospel continues the story. The ritual is based upon the lived experience of Jesus in the world, with his disciples and those who came to believe in him. In John's gospel there is no specific ritual of the breaking of the bread and the sharing of the cup at the Last Supper. Instead, there is another eucharistic ritual, another telling of the story: the ritual of the washing of the feet of the disciples by Jesus. Both rituals are rooted in the same reality. For John's community—and for all the church—getting down on our knees in humble obedience, following Jesus' example of a lifetime of serving and performing those tasks that are needed in the world, is remembering Jesus, putting him back into our communities and uniting us as a holy people belonging to God.

The story is simple. Jesus intends to show his disciples how much he has loved them before he leaves them. He will love them and us to the end, as he passes through the doors of bloody death returning to his Father. So first, he stoops, bending before them, reversing the relationships. He, the master, washes their feet. This is the way to honor God, by honoring one another, and especially those among us in need of healing, care, and tenderness, let alone justice, freedom, and hope of living at long last as human beings.

Jesus comes to Simon Peter. Sometimes we read just the name Simon—his name before he met and encountered Jesus. At other times it is simply Peter—who he is after being converted to Jesus and the Kingdom. And at other times, like tonight, it is Simon Peter, where he is of both minds and hearts, acting more as he was before he followed Jesus, yet in the presence of Jesus, who renamed him. He resists: "Lord, are you going to wash my feet?" And Peter is told that he does not understand what Jesus does to him and for him in this gesture of obedience and submission. He resists more forcefully: "You will never wash my feet!" Jesus is patient and yet persistent: "If I don't wash you, you will have no share in my heritage." It is time for Peter to reconsider, and when he does he lunges forward in his typical way: "Not only my feet, but my hands and head as well."

Our society is out of touch with such rituals of hospitality, welcome, service, and honor, and so the depth of what is happening and the reasoning behind Peter's outburst often go unrealized. Washing a person's feet was onerous work. People wore, at most, sandals in a world of heat, loose garbage, and animal droppings. People's feet were crusted, smelly, and repulsive, and even worse if they were diseased or had sores. Even husbands could not demand that their wives wash their feet. It was something that was necessary, but it was done as a courtesy, an honor for a guest arriving in a host's house, or in love, affection, dedication, or service, expressing a relationship of obedience and submission freely given. Sometimes disciples washed their master's feet, an honor that expressed a level of trust and intimacy between the two, but never did the master wash the disciples' feet. Never! This is more than the reversal of fortunes so often spoken of and proclaimed in the good news. This is a reversal of what constitutes worship of God. Submission, obedience, service, bending before others is bending before God, because now, in the mystery of the incarnation, we do indeed bend before God when we serve one another's needs and tend to one another's wounds.

The way the story is told, Judas is mentioned twice: once at the beginning, already intending to hand Jesus over; and again, in his effect on the community: "not all are washed clean." But there is the sense that Judas is present and that he, too, has his feet washed. Jesus bends before him humbly, touching his feet, knowing that he himself will be handled more roughly because of the callousness and treachery of this man he has called his friend. Whom do we refuse to bend before, knowing what they have done, what they intend to do to us? Whom do we resist when they come before us to serve? Whom would we rather not bend before and wash their feet? *All* must be included in this intimate gesture that takes place around the table of the Lord.

After washing their feet, Jesus reclines once again at the table and asks them: "Do you understand what I just did for you? You address me as 'Teacher' and 'Lord,' and fittingly enough, for that is what I am. But if I washed your feet—I who am your Teacher and Lord—then you must wash each other's feet. What I just did was to give you an example: as I have done, so you must do." This ritual is not just a momentary or one-time experience to impress upon the disciples the depth of Jesus' love for them. It is a moment that ritualizes and intensifies his entire life and the love that is at the root of all his actions.

This night is about bread and wine, about bodies and blood, about feet and washing, about intimacy and unbounded, unexpected love, about a God who bends before us hoping that one day we will treat each other with the same regard and dignity that he has always lavished upon us. This is what the new covenant is about. This is what worship is about. This is what reality and religion are about. This is what community and love are about.

Some theologians and preachers say that basically Jesus was killed because of the way he ate, whom he ate with, and what he encouraged them to do with one another as sign of their allegiance to him and to the Kingdom of his Father.

There is an old story told among Zen teachers.

✢ Once upon a time there was a family, the relatives of a poor sick samurai, who were dying of hunger. They approached Eisai's temple, and the good monk there took the golden halo off the image of the Buddha and gave it to them, telling them to go and sell it and buy food for themselves and find shelter. When others heard about it there was the cry of "Sacrilege!" What reckless and dangerous behavior! What kind of precedent was set for the temples!

But the monk calmly reminded them of the story of the Chinese master Tanka, who burned a wooden image to warm himself. And he preached to them: Buddha's mind is full of love and mercy. If the Buddha had heard the plight of these people, why, he would have cut off a limb if that would have helped them in their pain! What's a halo or anything else that's available in the face of human beings' suffering and need?

We are invited to eat and drink at the table of the Lord, to have our feet washed, to enter the wounds and heart of Christ, to be as his beloved friends. And we are told to do as Jesus did. We must wash each other's feet. Jesus expressed his love in service to the world. Now that is our task.

Good Friday

The Passion of the Lord

Isaiah 52:13-53:12
Hebrews 4:14-16, 5:7-9
John 18:1-19:42

The long portion from Isaiah is a lament, a commentary on the suffering that we can endure at one another's hands. It tells the anguished story of all those tortured, persecuted, and subjected to violence. It is brutal and unrelenting as it seeks to break past our defenses and inertia and touch our belief and hearts.

It is very effective when read by a number of people slowly and solemnly, as one would read the names of the dead in a litany of remembrance. The last portion must be proclaimed with confidence; it is the announcement of belief and faith even in the face of the hideous destruction of a human being. It acknowledges the one who suffers and his undying hope in God in his sufferings, and it proclaims that this kind of suffering redeems and justifies others. In bearing others' guilt Jesus endures death but takes away the sins of many and wins pardon for the offenses of others.

This day is not just about Jesus' suffering and death, a legal but unjust execution. It is about us and our share in his sacrifice in behalf of others. We share in the blessings that result from the suffering of Christ, and we must be sure that we do not contribute to or allow the destruction of others.

We are mortal. We will die, but death does not define us. It is built into the structure of our lives, institutions, and relationships, but what defines us is life, life born of witness to and sharing in the life of Christ. Because Jesus has suffered with us, sharing in our human mortality and our connection to one another, all suffering can be etched in dignity and given the power of God in Jesus.

Commitment to the Kingdom of Jesus, to the person of Jesus, invariably places us at the heart of the suffering of the world. Do we choose to ease the suffering and take down human beings from their crosses, resisting those who would destroy others? Or do we stand with those who see violence toward others as a viable strategy? We must choose.

Today we are confronted with the cross. It is held up for us to look at, to bend before and honor and kiss, to share its power to redeem. We are invited to sink into the mystery of a crucified God whose love shares even in the brutality we visit upon one another yet cries out NO! God suffered in Jesus, but God continues to suffer in millions of people caught in the forces of hate. We must confront the cross and Christ in those among us who suffer.

After such a description of evil, we need silence in which to situate ourselves with the victims, with God in Jesus, and to make sure that we are not allied with those who kill or profit from the death and suffering of others. Then, and only then, can we pray "Father, I put my life in your hands." We must remember all those who are forgotten, all those who are broken, all those who fall into the clutches of their enemies and persecutors. We commend ourselves and them to God, vowing with God's help to rescue them, to have courage and hope in the Lord by standing with Jesus, the crucified One, in spirit and in the flesh of others in history. Our ritual and our prayer must proclaim what we intend to do with our energy and power, with our united spirits and the power of God in Jesus, who put his life in the hands of God while the hands of hate nailed him down and marked the wood with his blood.

The letter to the Hebrews tells us our high priest sympathizes with our weakness and was tempted in every way, yet never sinned. We can confidently approach the throne of grace—the cross—to receive mercy and favor and find help in time of need. We are reminded that Christ suffered as we do and yet offered supplications in his agony with tears and loud cries to God. And he was heard, as the cry of the poor and the prophet alike are heard, especially because of his unfailing reverence and obedience to God. We are all human with Jesus, but human now in ways that confound the world and save it. We suffer because we are human and too often because of our sins and the sins of others. The consequences of sin are rampant in the world, affecting us all.

But we are reminded: "Son though he was, he learned obedience from what he suffered; and when perfected, he became the source of eternal salvation for all who obey him.' We, the sons and daughters of the Father, the brothers and sisters of the crucified One, learn obedience from our sufferings. Some of us suffer very little, and others suffer terribly, without support or affirmation even from those who claim to share the company of Jesus. Suffering can destroy those without faith, but suffering bound to Jesus can redeem, give dignity to suffering, and restore others to life and holiness. All the pain and suffering of the world are bound in the flesh of Jesus. Once tied to his body and blood, we can disappear into the wounds of Jesus and know that we too "will see the light in the fullness of days."

John's account of the passion of Jesus is different from that of the other writers. It begins with the betrayal in the garden, where Jesus stands before the Roman soldiers and the Jewish Temple police and asks, "Whom are you looking for?" They fall back before him. His power is spiritual, not physical, and certainly not violent. He turns on Peter, who had drawn his sword, and tells him to put it up. He has chosen his way, and violence has no part in it. It is better, holier, to know pain rather than to inflict it on others. And so Jesus is bound and led away.

The trial follows, and Peter betrays Jesus three times vehemently, afraid for his own skin. Jesus is taken to Pilate, for his enemies are seeking the death penalty. Pilate interrogates Jesus, and Jesus is forthright and without subterfuge. When asked if he is a king, Jesus turns the question back on Pilate. And when questioned about his Kingdom, he answers: "My Kingdom does not belong to this world. If my Kingdom were of this world, my subjects would be fighting to save me from being handed over to the Jews. As it is, my Kingdom is not here." Jesus is a king, but radically different from anything the kingdoms of the world have ever seen or known. He continues: "It is you who say I am a king. The reason I was born, the reason why I came into the world, is to testify to the truth. Anyone committed to the truth hears my voice." This is the essence of Jesus, his person, work, relation to the Father, place in the world, and place in the realm of the Spirit. Truth. No matter what is done to him, he will speak and be the truth of God. He testifies. He witnesses to God. He is martyred for the truth. He is "disappeared."

Pilate is convinced by the people. He has Jesus scourged, crowned, and mocked by his soldiers. Then he questions Jesus again. This time the issue is power: Pilate's power to kill Jesus or let him live, and Jesus' power to lay down his life and let them kill him. Jesus' explanation is not easy to comprehend: "You would have no power over me whatever unless it were given you from above. That is why he who handed me over to you is guilty of the greater sin." The misuse of power is sin. The use of power to kill, to destroy is a sin. And when that power is misused by those who are connected religiously to Jesus, it is an even greater sin.

Finally Pilate hands Jesus over to be crucified, and crucified as king, between two others. His garments are divided among his executioners, but for his seamless cloak they throw dice.

There are witnesses in John's gospel: his mother, his mother's sister, Mary the wife of Clopas, Mary Magdalene, and John, the disciple that Jesus loved. His mother is given to the disciple and the disciple in turn is handed over to the mother. This is the new family of Jesus. And it is seamless, united, a universal family, symbolized by the inscription, which is written in Hebrew, Latin, and Greek. The relationships are intimate, defying blood or marriage ties. The ties are those of the blood of the cross, sacrifice, and being given to each other for care-taking.

Jesus thirsts and is offered wine with hyssop to drink. When he drinks, he speaks his last words: "It is finished." Then he bows his head and delivers over his spirit. His thirst has been constant all his life: for the will and honor of God, for the truth to be told and given a place of honor in the world, for the Kingdom of God to come upon earth, for people who are believers. Now his work is done. His last gift to his father is his spirit, his life, his love: everything.

Immediately the world kicks in and tries to take over. It is the preparation day for the sabbath, and the Jews don't want the bodies left hanging there during the religious prayers and rites. So the legs of the others are broken to hasten their death. Because Jesus is already dead, his side is pierced by a lance and blood and water flow out. The church is born in that gushing forth of blood and water from the side of Jesus. With his last breath the Spirit of God was let loose in the world, free to seep into every corner and crevice of the universe. The resurrection has begun as Jesus' blood seeps into the earth and his breath disappears into the air. Jesus is buried quickly, with haste and no undue attention, wrapped in spices that weighed about a hundred pounds. He is buried in a garden, in a new tomb, and left. Jesus disappears into the earth. Jesus disappears into the arms and heart of his Father. It is done.

We gather to listen to the end, hear the story, kiss the cross, and pray for the entire world. We gather to stand silent before death, sin, and evil and to acknowledge our part in the destruction of Jesus and the continued destruction of human beings and the world that God has created. We stand at the foot of the cross as onlookers, witnesses, disciples—part of the new family of God, crucified, bound to each other in common shared grief and the exhortation to care for one another, especially for those who are broken and in need. We stand in the shadow of the cross, grieving but intent on not allowing this to continue. The cross is our salvation, but it is so much more.

We bear the cross with Christ. We are marked with its sign as saving grace and as belonging to the Son of Man, who was judged, condemned, and murdered. He will come again in glory to judge the living and the dead with justice born of suffering and obedience to God alone. We mark ourselves with the sign of the cross and begin and end our prayers with it. Ezekiel put a mark on the foreheads of all those who sought to honor God and who prayed in anguish over the abominations and sin committed in Jerusalem before the coming of judgment (Ezekiel 9:4). And the book of Revelation tells of the servants of God being sealed on their foreheads before the day of destruction and the coming of judgment (7:3). At our baptisms we are signed with oil, and those who bring us to the fount sign us with the cross, drawing us into the company of Christ.

Death can be tragic, horrible, and even meaningless. Jesus' violent death was expedient, useful, seen as necessary to the powers in control, contrived. He was betrayed, condemned through false witness, and executed according to the capital punishment laws of his days. It was legal; it was unjust.

But death is only meaningless and without redemption when it is separate from the death of Christ. There is more death in those who kill, obeying the powers of the world, than in the death of those who seek to be human and to be truthful. We are commanded to resist death without dignity, without meaning, death that is legal but unnecessary.

But our ways of fighting are as strange as the cross. They are to be the weapons of nonviolent resistance, of communities that offer hope to the victims of injustice, of tender mercies, of offering ourselves as hostage, of working for justice, of living with and choosing the company of the poor and the outcast, and of prayer and love for all, even our enemies. Scratched on the wall of a concentration camp in Germany were these words:

> Lord, remember not only the men and women of good will but all those of ill will. Do not only remember all the suffering they have subjected us to. Remember the fruits we brought forth thanks to this suffering—our comradeship, our loyalty, our humility, our courage and generosity, the greatness of heart that all of this inspired. And when they come to judgment, let all these fruits we have borne be their reward and their forgiveness.

This is the cross. This is Good Friday. This is salvation.

We leave the church in silence. Jesus is dead. It is finished. Now is the time of loss and emptiness, the in-between time of death and resurrection. The seed is in the ground, and with time it will sprout and break forth from the tomb and burst into bloom. For now, though, there is nothing. The presence of God in Jesus has disappeared. Nothing is left, no trace but a stone rolled in front of a tomb, a blood-soaked cross, torn garments, a crown of thorns, and memories. Have we disappeared? What is left of us? What will God have to work on? It seems that resurrection is born most surely of nothingness, of matter that has disappeared into spirit, of flesh that is sacrificed and offered to God. What more do we need to let go of? Perhaps one more story and all that needs to go will disappear.

This is a story from Brazil. It was told by one of my students and friends, Brian O'Sullivan:

✛ Once upon a time there was a poor peasant family that had worked for years scrimping and saving to buy a piece of land of its own. Finally the day came, and they took possession of it. The mother and half a dozen children gathered in the two-room shack that would serve as their house, while the father walked the length and breadth of their land. He paced it out, marking the four corners as boundaries, praying in joy and thanksgiving as he walked. As he rounded the last corner and laid the stone in place he noticed something sticking out from under a bush.

He bent and scratched at the dirt, digging with his hands, and soon unearthed the corpus from a crucifix. It had obviously been in the ground a long time. Its hands and arms were gone, and its feet and legs missing. It was mangled, scratched, cracked, the paint nearly all gone. He picked it up and carried it back in his arms to the house. It was a good size corpus. The crucifix it hung on must have been ten or twelve feet tall. He came in and laid it on the kitchen table.

The family stood around it, looking at it, in an awkward silence. The father explained that he had found it on their land. It was the first thing he had dug out of the ground. What should they do with it? Should they take it to the church and give it to the padre? Should they burn it? Should they bury it again? They all stood and looked at it.

Finally, the youngest spoke: "Father, I have an idea."

"What, my child?"

"Why don't we hang it on the kitchen wall and put a sign underneath it."

"What would you put on the sign?"

And the youngest told them.

There was a long silence. Then the corpus was hung with care on the whitewashed wall of the kitchen and a small sheet of paper was tacked underneath. It read: "Jesus has no arms or legs. Will you lend him yours?"

The memory of Jesus is dangerous, subversive, death-threatening, life-affirming, bursting with hope, and mindful of evil. It is not naive but born of faith and community, the community that stands at the foot of the cross, overshadowed by it, turned toward the tomb, expectant. We leave the church, the tomb, our past behind us, and we go out into the world and wait. Jesus lies in the arms of his Father. His passion is over, passed on to us now. We mourn our loss of his presence among us, but we remember, and we pray:

> *The tree of the cross has become for us*
> *a plant of endless well-being:*
> *it gives us our nourishment;*
> *we strike root in its roots*

and in its branches we spread;
its dew is our joy
and its rustling makes us prolific.
—Anonymous

It is Good Friday.

The Easter Vigil

Easter: The Resurrection of the Lord

Genesis 1:1-2:2

This is the night of storytelling. It begins with gathering around the Easter candle, the light of Christ, to remember our past and where we came from, who we are, and the wonder of God, who has been at work since the beginning of creation. Our roots are all good, very good.

We are bound together, intimately connected, all created by the One who blesses us and tells us to have dominion over the earth as God has dominion over us. It happened as the Word of God, the spirit and breath of God, spoke and it was all very good.

We are made to please God.

Genesis 22:1-18

Our beginning in faith is just as auspicious.

Abraham is called, singled out by God, and put to the test. God wants all that Abraham holds dear, including his beloved son. In anguish and confusion Abraham obeys; he goes to the mountain with Isaac and begins to sacrifice his child. But God is the God of life; there is to be no sacrifice of human beings to God, who is the mystery of all time and life. God wants obedience, surrender, and a life handed over to him alone, trusting that all will be given as needed.

We all begin on that mountain with Abraham, learning to worship truly and hearing the promises of the future echoing in our ears.

Exodus 14:15-15:1

This is the central reading of the vigil: the passing through the Red Sea, with the waters parted by God. The Egyptians in pursuit are caught in the waters of death, while the Israelites are drawn forth into freedom.

The power of God is shown in the Lord's works, in the choice of the children of Israel, and in the waters that redeem and lead to hope and community. The enemies of God, those who imprison, oppress, and destroy others, are judged and in the hands of God. God is on the side of those who pass through the waters.

Isaiah 54:5-14

God seeks intimacy with the beloved people, Israel, as a husband draws near to his beloved wife. There is reconciliation and tenderness in all God's experiences with the chosen people, who are more often than not unfaithful and insensitive to God, refusing to allow God entrance into their hearts.

God's love is enduring. It never leaves us. When we are storm-battered, afflicted, and inconsolable, God approaches to embrace us and establish us with justice and peace where no destruction can come near us again.

Isaiah 55:1-11

This is an announcement: come all who are thirsty, poor, indebted, hungry, and be filled. Come! God will always renew us with life, nation, home, and the glory of God, which will shine throughout us for others to see.

Seek God while God is near, easily found, and seek mercy because God is generous and forgiving. God is not like us. God's thought is not like ours. Yahweh's words come like rain and snow to water the earth, nourishing the seed and yielding the harvest. They do not return to God empty but filled. The divine will is achieved. What God sends upon the earth will do what it was sent to do. Jesus sent upon the earth will obey God, and life abundant will be brought forth from the seed that is the Word of God.

Baruch 3:9-15, 32-4:4

Hear the commands and know life, even in the midst of exile, dread, and having forsaken the wisdom of God. We can learn prudence, strength, and understanding even when we have walked away from God. We must learn to know wisdom, her treasures and life, her knowledge and light, the mysteries of the universe and stars.

God has traced out this way of understanding and given it to us. Wisdom has appeared on the earth and moved among us. She is the book of law and all who cling to her live. Receive her. What pleases God is known to us. It is given as a gift. Accept it.

Ezekiel 36:16-28

Son of man, I have scattered my people among the nations because they are sinners, defile my Temple, and insult me, and I have judged them. And I have relented because of my Holy Name.

Even when you do not honor me, I remember you and I will act on your behalf and bring you home and I will prove my holiness through you! I will gather you back and sprinkle clean water on you (baptism) and cleanse you and put a new spirit into your stony hearts (confirmation) and I will let you live in the land I gave you and you will be my people (eucharist) and I will be your God.

It is time to come home again.

Romans 6:3-11

With this reading, after the singing of the Gloria and the ringing of the bells and the coming of the light in the church, we are reminded of who we are and what has been done for us in Jesus: "Are you not aware that we who were baptized into Christ Jesus were baptized into his death? Through baptism into his death we were buried with him, so that, just as Christ was raised from the dead by the glory of the Father, we too might live a new life."

We have been crucified; all is destroyed. Our old lives have disappeared, and we are slaves to sin no longer. Death has no power now over Christ and no power over us. "His death was death to sin, once for all; his life is life for God. In the same way, you must consider yourselves dead to sin but alive for God in Christ Jesus." This is the heart of the mystery of Jesus' death and resurrection.

We are alive for the glory of God and we live in Christ. We have no life of our own anymore. All of that has disappeared. Our only response for fifty days is Alleluia! Alleluia! Alleluia!

Matthew 28:1-10

Resurrection! It happens in the dark with no witnesses, just the Father bending over the Son and breathing the Spirit back into his flesh. And everything is shattered. The sabbath is over. It is the first day of the week, the eighth day of the week. It is the new creation, and it is just dawning.

Two women come to inspect the tomb: Mary Magdalene and the other Mary. There is an earthquake, and the angel of the Lord descends from heaven. The stone is rolled back, and the angel sits on it. His appearance is a flash of lightning and his garments dazzling as snow. The guards are paralyzed with fear and fall down like dead men. The women are stronger; they stand there, and the angel speaks to them: "Do not be frightened. I know you are looking for Jesus the crucified, but he is not here."

He has been raised, exactly as he promised. "Come and see the spot where he was laid. Then go quickly and tell his disciples: 'He has been raised from the dead and now goes ahead of you to Galilee, where you will see him.' That is the message I have for you."

Matthew's account of the resurrection is very different from the other gospels. There is this angel with the announcement of the end and beginning. There is the violent and physical interruption of the earth, the tomb, and the soldiers, with heaven breaking into history.

The message is proclaimed. It has all the traditional elements of dealing with the power of God: an angel descends, brightness, and the opening words: "Do not be afraid." Resurrection happens when simple grieving people are on their way to inspect the realms of death, seeking the crucified One, Jesus.

But we will not find Jesus in tombs or in any place that is ruled by violence, self-satisfaction, greed, or any institution that deals in death and lies. We find him out in the world, specifically in Galilee, that is, among the poor, the workers, those struggling for a way to survive in an unjust world, our neighbors, believers and unbelievers alike, whom we have known and who have known us always. We will see him there.

Resurrection sends Jesus back into the world, and it sends us back into the world, unafraid now, still seeking the crucified One who is now raised up in glory and hidden in our midst. The women hurry away from the tomb "half-overjoyed, half-fearful," and they go to carry the good news. They are evangelizers carrying the word of life, hope, new creation. There is life after death, the power of evil and violence is broken, light and dazzling possibilities abound. And as they run, there is Jesus standing right in front of them, without any warning. They could have run right into him! Jesus' first word of resurrection is "Peace!" They embrace his feet and do him homage. And he tells them "Do not be afraid! Go and carry the news to my brothers that they are to go to Galilee, where they will see me."

They carry the news and they pass on the story, the words and the command: Go! Go back to your homes and work. Go back to your families and relatives and friends and neighbors and enemies. Go and find God there. Go to the world of commerce, economics, politics. Seek out the poor and those who search for God and go looking with them. That's where he was before. That's where he is now. We touch the feet of the One who has suffered and been crucified and do him homage and obey, returning to those he knelt before and did homage to, honoring them as ones cherished by his Father.

The good news goes first to his brothers and friends. His sisters carry it forth and are told not to be afraid—of anything or anyone! They are to go with peace. Peace is the undeniable presence of the Risen Lord. Peace, not as the world gives, but peace that knows what sin and evil can do, the scars it leaves behind, but also knows the life that is unquenchable within and the Spirit that is irrepressible and indestructible.

This story is ours too. Peace to all of us who have come seeking the crucified One, now risen in glory. We bend and embrace his feet and do him homage. Then we run into the world and spread the good news to our friends, to whom we are bound in baptism and the Spirit. Then we go out into the wider world, to our Galilee, our cities and outskirts of the realms of power, and seek him there. We find him where he is most at home—among the poor and those who struggle for dignity and a life that death cannot tear apart.

Today we proclaim that we believe in the resurrection. What is resurrection? In *Blessed Are You Who Believed*, Carlo Carretto describes resurrection this way:

> When the world seems a defeat for God and you are sick with the disorder, the violence, the terror, the war on the streets; when the earth seems to be chaos, say to yourself, "Jesus died and rose again on purpose to save, and his salvation is already with us."
>
> When your father or your mother, your son or your daughter, your spouse or your friend are on their death-bed, and you are looking at them in the pain of parting, say, "We shall see each other again in the Kingdom; courage . . ."
>
> Every departing missionary is an act of faith in the resurrection.
>
> Every newly-opened leper-hospital is an act of faith in the resurrection.
>
> Every peace treaty is an act of faith in the resurrection.
>
> Every agreed commitment is an act of faith in the resurrection.
>
> When you forgive your enemy
> When you feed the hungry
> When you defend the weak
> you believe in the resurrection.
>
> When you have the courage to marry
> When you welcome the newly-born child
> When you build your home
> you believe in the resurrection.

When you wake at peace in the morning
When you sing to the rising sun
When you go to work with joy
you believe in the resurrection.

Friedrich Nietzsche, a nineteenth-century philosopher, wrote about Christians and Christianity. He praised Christianity as a religion but he never became a Christian. His answer when questioned about this: "For a group of people who claim to believe in resurrection, none of them looks redeemed!"

The undeniable sign of resurrection is joy, looking redeemed, bringing a sense of hope to others that is tangible and irresistible. It is not shallow but deep, abiding, and enduring. Death cannot break its hold, and suffering and persecution often strengthen it. It brings light and remembers to seek out the stars in the darkest part of night. It is hard-nosed self-sacrifice, knowledgeable of the razor edge of sin, and yet it knows when to sidestep, when to dance, and when to run—and when to stand face to face and stare evil down and take its knife thrust. It is the work of reconciliation, and it abhors violence and insensitivity to others' pain. It knows fear but is not paralyzed or controlled by it. It feeds on the word and trusts in the blood and shares the bread graciously with all. It shoulders the cross and denies itself and turns toward the face of God in all others. It announces the victory of justice and grasps our hand for that victory in our life and wrests us free of the grip of evil and isolation. It thrives in community, and when it is alone it is at home in the larger Kingdom of God's realm and the Trinity.

It belongs to all the world and will not honor any one nation or philosophy or group over another, except perhaps those who have no power: the poor. It exalts in the cross and honors those who suffer on behalf of others, closest to the Christ here and now. It hides out, outside the gates, outside the realms of power and institutions, even outside of church, and it hides in mystery and silence. Our lives are proclamations: "We shall not die but live and declare the works of the Lord."

The stone that the builders rejected has become
the cornerstone.

By the Lord has this been done and it is
wonderful in our eyes. (Psalm 118)

Perhaps a story tells it best. It is a story from Persia, a
Muslim tale called "The Two Beggars."

✢ Once upon a time there were two beggars. One day they
decided to take their chances and beg from the king himself.

They went straight up to the windows of the palace
where he was deciding upon laws and seeing to the up-
keep of his land, and they started crying out. They
pleaded and begged, in the name of Allah, the most com-
passionate one, in the name of mercy, even praising the
king himself in hopes of something. Finally, to get rid of
them, the king went to the window and had his servants
throw them some bread.

Immediately one of the beggars broke into praise of
the king, blessing him, singing his praises, and the king
smiled. The other, however, ignored the king and broke
into song praising Allah for his compassion and mercy
and graciousness. The king was annoyed and yelled out
at him: "Why do you praise Allah for what I give you? It
is I who give to you."

The beggar looked at him and said, "You only give
because it was first given to you by Allah to distribute."
The king was annoyed, and the two beggars eventually
drifted away to eat their bread.

The next day they decided to try again. Back they
went and again set up such a din that the king was infu-
riated. He threw bread and a few coins at them and had
them taken from the area. Again, one beggar praised
him and the other praised only Allah.

Again the king became angry, and this time he decided
to do something about it. He went downstairs to the kitch-
ens and had two loaves of bread made, exactly alike. In
one he put a small cache of jewels; in the other, just dough.

The next day the beggars were back, as he suspected
they would be, and he was ready. To the beggar who
praised him, he gave the loaf with the jewels. To the beg-

gar who praised Allah, he gave the ordinary bread. They left to eat.

On the way to a cooler, quieter spot outside the city, the beggar with the loaf loaded with the jewels noticed his bread was heavy. He thought to himself, This bread must be as hard as a rock. I'll see if this man will trade loaves with me. So, he spoke: "My friend," he said, "this loaf seems very well done, firm, just the way you prefer your bread Would you like to switch loaves?" And so, they switched loaves of bread.

The beggar who now had the plain loaf of bread made his excuses and went off to eat by himself. The other beggar, the one who praised Allah, took his loaf, as he was wont, to a large tree outside the city, where he often shared his bread with those who hadn't fared as well in their begging ventures. He sat and tore into the bread, giving pieces to others and found the jewels inside! Again he praised Allah profusely and shared the jewels with other beggars.

The next day there was just one beggar at the king's window. When the king looked down he was amazed to find it was the "wrong" beggar, the one to whom he had given jewels hidden in the dough. "What are you doing here? Where is the other beggar? What did you do with the loaf I gave you yesterday?"

The man replied, "I am begging as I always do. I don't know where the other is. He never showed up today. There have been stories of him coming into better times. I gave him the loaf you gave me. It was heavy, lumpy, and I knew it wouldn't taste good. He gladly switched with me."

The king was humbled. The beggar who praised Allah was vindicated. No matter what the king had plotted, Allah had other ideas and had used even his pettiness and meanness, even his arrogance, to change the world's outcomes. And he thought to himself: Perhaps he was right on the other issue as well. Perhaps I only have what I have to give because Allah had given it to me to distribute.

They say there weren't many beggars in the kingdom after a while, and the king was devoted to the praise of Allah.

We are all beggars in the Kingdom of God. The praise of God must be ever in our mouths, for the power of God extends and rests deep in history as the cache of jewels hidden in the dough. In the fullness of time all will be laid bare and all will know the power of God that we name resurrection.

The second reading from the Mass for Easter day is about dough, about yeast. We are reminded today to get rid of the old yeast and to make of ourselves fresh dough. We are to disappear now into the dough. Christ our Passover has been sacrificed. We are to celebrate the feast with the new bread of sincerity and truth. Come, let us eat the Body of Christ and take up the cup filled with the wine of salvation and toast the life and death of the Lord with the closing lines of the Easter sequence:

> Christ indeed from death is risen, our new life
>   obtaining.
> Have mercy, victor King, ever reigning!
> Amen. Alleluia.

Now, as we begin to live in sincerity and truth, we should remember the words of Daniel Berrigan:

> Sometime in your life, hope that you might
>   see one starved man, the look on his face
>   when the bread finally arrives.
> Hope that you might have baked it or bought
>   it or even kneaded it yourself.
> For that look on his face, for your meeting his
>   eyes across a piece of bread, you might be
>   willing to lose a lot, or suffer a lot, or die a
>   little, even.

In losing it all we gain life, ever more abundant life. When everything else disappears only Love remains, only God. This is why we tell all the stories. The Word is true. Alleluia.